Ordinary People,

Extraordinary Faith

Ordinary People, Extraordinary Faith

STORIES OF INSPIRATION

JONI EARECKSON TADA

WITH KAY STROM

A JANET THOMA BOOK

THOMAS NELSON PUBLISHERS
Nashville

TO

RYAN MAZZA,

WHO KEEPS LEADING THE WAY

∽

Contents

⌒

Ordinary People,

Extraordinary Faith

Now faith is being sure of what we hope for and certain of what we do not see.

HEBREWS 11:1

ORDINARY PEOPLE,
EXTRAORDINARY FAITH

*N*ot but two minutes ago, after hacking and coughing, I turned to Francie, my secretary, and confessed, "I'm feeling a little blue today." A weeklong bout with the flu hadn't helped my spirits, and coming back to my office to face piles of work on my desk hadn't helped either. And so, after fits and starts at the computer, my shoulders started slumping.

"Okay," I admitted, "I'm downright depressed."

Then I spotted the perky bouquet of flowers that had arrived earlier in the day and said with much contrition, "Wait a minute. What in the world do I have to be depressed about?!"

My friend Karla Larson—bless her heart—heard I'd been under the weather and sent me the flowers. *I'm* the one who should be sending Karla gifts. A severe condition of diabetes is at the root of her problems—she has suffered a heart attack, a kidney transplant, the amputation of both legs. She is legally blind, has endured countless angioplasties, and has lost several fingers. I wrote about Karla in my book *When God Weeps,* explaining that when I met her at one of our Joni and Friends Family Retreats, I said, "Karla, I can't believe you were able to make it," to which she replied, "I thought I'd better come

My husband, Ken, and me at the Joni and Friends Family Retreat with our faithful friend Karla Larson and her attendant, Priscilla

before I lost any more body parts." She has not lost her sense of humor.

I think of Karla when I'm asked, "Who inspires you? Who are your role models?" My mind, like a computer, sorts through a list of possibilities, but I always come up with ordinary people like her.

I also think of the women who get me up in the morning. What inspirations they are to me! There are eight different girls who, on seven different mornings, come to my house at 7:30 A.M. to fix coffee, put my legs through exercises, give me a bed bath, get me dressed, and sit me up in my wheelchair. These are average women, the kind who stand in line in front of you at Wal-Mart or whom you run into at Starbucks. They are a seamstress, a hairstylist, a bookkeeper, a secretary, a data entry supervisor, a mother and daughter, and an administrator. They have homes and family members, mortgage payments, and kitchen appliance problems. Yet one has had an abortion and another is divorced and a cancer survivor. One is a recovering alcoholic. Another has a husband with Parkinson's and, when she isn't at the office, she tends to aging parents and a mother-in-law. One is an ex-hippie who used to do drugs. Another is a single woman in her sixties.

> *How do we take this measure of faith God gives us and make it extraordinary? It's all a matter of focus.*

Why are these women so inspiring to me? Partly because of the care they so selflessly give me. But even more because they hold on to God for dear life and confess daily their drastic need of Him.

Ordinary people . . . extraordinary faith.

I used to think it was wrong to ascribe different levels to people's faith, as though some were better than others. But Jesus did. He said of one individual in Matthew 14:31, "You of little faith . . ." and then a chapter later He said, "Woman, you have great faith!" Yet it has nothing to do with one person being better than the next. The apostle Paul wrote in Romans 12:3, "Do not think of yourself more highly than you ought, but rather think of yourself with sober judgment, *in accordance with the measure of faith God has given you*" (emphasis added).

Faith, you see, is a gift from God. And, really, it's not the size of that faith that matters. Jesus says your faith could be the size of a mustard seed and great things could still happen.

How do we take this measure of faith God gives us and make it . . . extraordinary? It's all a matter of focus. "Faith is being sure of what we hope for and certain of what we do not see" (Heb. 11:1). So faith is being sure of something you hope for—that is, sure about unfulfilled things in the future. And it's being certain of something you can't see—that is, being keenly aware of the unseen divine realities all around you.

The girls who help me get up and do my exercises in the morning

Faith makes that which is unseen, real. And that which is seen, much less important.

Great faith means focusing on the King and His kingdom priorities.

Karla lives this way. And so do the girls who get me up. When I observe *how* they hold on to God for dear life and confess daily their drastic need of Him, it makes me want to do the same. After all, we're together on the same team. We are in the minor leagues down here on earth, training for the major leagues in heaven. Each of us has been given a measure of faith and, with it, we train ourselves in godliness. We work with the equipment God has given us, stretching our faith muscles. And what happens when He calls you up to the plate and pitches you a fastball? You *connect*. You hit a line drive, if not a home run. You make it your ambition to be pleasing to Him (see 2 Cor. 5:9).

Some of us forget we're in training, though. We don't always think about the unseen divine realities happening all around us, and we certainly don't focus on heaven as we should. This is why it helps to read the stories of average people who, despite many setbacks, are stepping up to the plate. They have taken the faith God has given them and stretched it, widened it, and deepened it. They have held their feet to the fire, punching and disciplining and beating their bodies into submission, as it were, to strengthen their faith. And they have come through with great lessons to share. They have learned to forgive when forgiveness seemed impossible, to believe and love and obey against all odds. And when they cannot see where and how God is leading, they have learned to wait on the Lord and to persevere and overcome. They have learned to be faithful and to serve selflessly for the glory of God, and to be strong through greater authority. They have learned the true meaning of freedom.

> *Faith is being certain of something you can't see—being keenly aware of the unseen divine realities all around you.*

They are ordinary people like you, and you are about to meet them in this book. I have selected fifteen friends for the purpose of sharing their stories of extraordinary faith. And I didn't have to look far.

It was not as though I sweated and labored, wondering just who "Joni's Top 15" might be. On the contrary, the friends in this book are a random sampling of average folks, just like the girls who get me up in the morning. What makes them special is their faith—or I should say the *focus* of their faith. They inspire those around them. They refresh those with whom they rub shoulders. Like Karla with her flowers, they help keep our faith focused.

Absolutely anyone—any believer in Christ—can have extraordinary faith. It's all a matter of focus, for "faith comes from hearing the message, and the message is heard through the word of Christ" (Rom. 10:17).

Come hear the message.

Come see the Word of Christ lived out in the lives of my fifteen friends.

It'll have you focusing on the King and His kingdom priorities. It'll have you on your way to greater faith.

For if you forgive men when they sin against you, your heavenly Father will also forgive you.

MATTHEW 6:14

2

Yet Will I Trust
Him . . . and Forgive

*I*t was thirteen years after my accident and I was finally beginning to accept my paralysis. After years of living with my sister Jay on her Maryland farm, I moved to California to start a ministry to help families affected by disability.

At the first ministry board meeting of the newly christened Joni and Friends, I met Dr. Sam Britten, who had started an outreach for disabled people at Grace Community Church. He was also the director of the Center of Achievement for the Physically Disabled at a

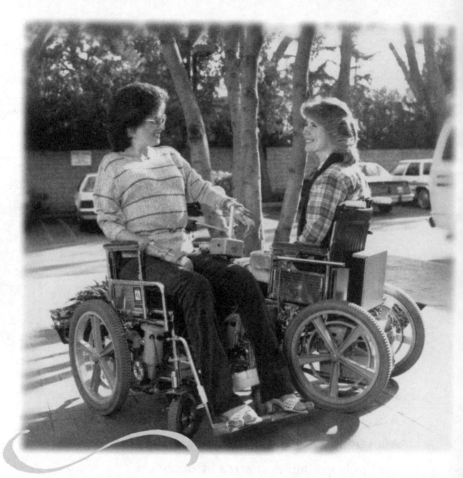

Vicky Olivas and me

nearby campus of California State University. He invited me to visit the center, and I did so the very next day.

In the main room, leg braces hung on the walls. Canes, crutches, and walkers were neatly lined up by the parallel bars at the far end of the room. Pulleys with weights covered one wall next to a floor-to-ceiling mirror. The room bustled with activity. Weights slammed, straps buckled, people chattered and laughed.

Earlier, when Dr. Britten first suggested I might be able to drive a van, I was dubious to say the least. But at his insistence I went through an evaluation process. Afterward he told me, "Looks great. I see no reason why you can't begin some simple strengthening exercises right now."

"Driving, huh?" I challenged him with an unbelieving smile. But I did begin working regularly on the exercise cycle.

Everyone was busy—everyone except one young woman who was sitting perfectly still in the corner, her arms propped on the wheelchair armrests. Her lovely Latin looks and mass of curly dark hair drew attention away from her wheelchair. An attendant spoke to her in Spanish, and I wondered whether it was her striking appearance or the distant way she observed the rest of us that set her apart so distinctly. And I couldn't help being intrigued by her almost tangible isolation.

As I met people and talked with them about my faith and my acceptance of my wheelchair, I repeatedly stole glances at the beautiful dark-haired woman who continued to sit like a statue. She paid no attention to me or to anyone else, just stared straight ahead with eyes that rarely seemed to blink.

One of those I did meet was Rana Leavell, who was working with Dr. Britten in order to earn a credential to teach physical education to disabled high school kids. I asked her about the beautiful mystery woman in the corner.

"Her name's Vicky Olivas," Rana said. "She's only been paralyzed a few years." Then she added quietly, "She's really had a rough time."

"I've seen her here and I've been praying for her," I told Rana.

"Praying?" Rana said with a laugh. "Yeah, well . . ." Abruptly changing the subject she said, "Let me get someone to take you off this cycle machine."

Sin should never surprise us. The surprise is that God forgives any of us.

I longed to meet Vicky, but days passed before I got a chance. Then one morning I spotted her in a secluded area outside, smoking in the shade. Here was my opportunity.

"We've both been so busy we haven't had a chance to talk," I began as I pushed up to her.

"Yes, I've noticed you, too." Her beautiful English was heavily accented with her native Spanish. She gazed at me with clear green eyes. Close up she was even more beautiful. Her hands were propped on a flowered pillow, nicely displaying her slender fingers and perfectly polished nails. Her jeans were ironed and starched to a sharp crease and on her feet she wore high-heeled sandals. Even her toenails were perfectly polished. Her attendant held her cigarette, giving her a puff when Vicky desired.

"What's your reason for coming to the center?" I asked.

She stared at me incredulously. "To get healed," she said. After an awkward pause she added, "Isn't that why you're here?"

I wasn't prepared for that. Yet I had been praying to get to know her, so this was an answer to prayer. "I'm just trying to strengthen whatever muscles I've got," I said truthfully. "If I get more in return, that would be great." I shrugged my shoulders and added, "Whatever God wants."

"God?" she asked. "My psychologist says it's all in my head."

"Your paralysis? In your head?"

Vicky Olivas looked down at her lovely lifeless hands. I realized I'd said too much too soon. I started to say that perhaps, yes, such things did happen . . . rarely, but . . .

"My psychologist says if I keep coming here I may snap out of it." She talked slowly, as though speaking was difficult. "I went to a hypnotist . . . that didn't work. The spiritist didn't work either."

At that, my heart twisted. This woman was even more mysterious than I'd thought.

"I was in Russia not long ago," Vicky volunteered. "I had read about research going on at an institute in Leningrad." She went on to describe a battery of people who gave her deep muscle massage, braced her legs to help her stand, and told her to concentrate on her fingers.

"I can do this." She leaned ever so slightly forward in her wheelchair and shrugged her shoulders. She was so proud of that small bit of movement, convinced, I suppose, that the trip to Russia really did help. "And I'll do more. I know I will." She tilted her head toward her attendant, giving her the signal that she was ready for another puff of the cigarette and a sip of coffee.

What a strange contradiction. Vicky's only goal was to be healed. And she was certain she would be. Yet she was doing nothing to develop the muscles she did have. She simply showed up at the center and sat passively in the corner and waited.

When I was again able to talk to Rana about Vicky, she bluntly asked, "What I'd like to know is, where was God when all the awful stuff happened to her?"

"What stuff?" I asked.

As I relaxed into the cool, damp towel folded under my neck, Rana told me Vicky's story.

Vicky's husband had walked out on her and their two-year-old son, Arturo. For the first time in her life, Vicky was faced with the challenge of getting a job to support herself and her little boy.

It wasn't easy.

When a woman from an employment agency called one Friday afternoon, she told Vicky, "This interview could open the door to a real opportunity for you." It was an inconvenient time, it required a long drive to take Arturo to her parents' house, and it meant she had to borrow money from the neighbors for gas in order to make the trip. Still, she hesitantly decided to go.

It wasn't an easy address to find. Everything in the neighborhood seemed to be factories. Finally Vicky got directions from the receptionist at another company. She parked her car at the curb, walked to the corner, and looked down a long dirty alley. The receptionist had told her it was the last door. Vicky hesitated. By now it was late afternoon and the place looked awfully forbidding. *Well,* she thought, *I've come this far. I may as well go through with the interview.*

Vicky opened the front door and stepped into the office. No one was there. She saw a typewriter, but it was covered with dust. The floor was strewn with paper, and the place had a damp, closed-in smell. She peeked around the corner and cautiously made her way down the hallway. "Hello?" she called. "Is anyone here? Hello?"

She walked on through the warehouse and came to another office where two men were sitting, one behind a scarred Formica desk and the other slouched in a molded plastic chair with his arms folded.

"My name is Vicky Olivas," she began uncertainly. "The employment agency sent me over."

The man behind the desk, obviously the boss, leaned back and looked her up and down. "Yes, I've been expecting you," he said. "Do you have a résumé?"

"No . . . no," she stammered. "Not with me."

He slid an application across the desk and ordered, "Here. Go into the front office and fill it out while I finish here."

Vicky, shaking slightly but resigned to seeing the interview through, obediently began to fill in her address and social security number. She glanced up and noticed two men unloading boxes into the warehouse. By the time they finished and pulled away, she had completed the form.

The owner entered the room, closing the door behind him, and fastened the lock. A chill of apprehension went down Vicky's spine.

"Let's go into my office," the man said. He motioned the way through a door and into another warehouse.

Then the nightmare began.

Suddenly the man grabbed her from behind and threw her against the wall. "Do you realize this is all planned?" he said. "I asked them to send somebody just like you. I've sent everyone else home. It's just us here."

He grabbed Vicky's blouse, and she squirmed violently to break free. Out of the corner of her eye she spotted the glint of something metal. A gun! Now, with every bit of her strength she wrestled to free herself.

Bang!

The room and the man spiraled round and round as Vicky slumped to the floor. Her thoughts spun out of control as she felt herself dragged over cold tiles. Where was he taking her? It was the bathroom! The filthy, smelly bathroom. She couldn't feel her legs. She strained to lift her arms, but she could not.

The man left the room, but in a few moments he returned. She could see him wipe his perspiring brow and nervously shake his head. Then he left, only to return and do the same thing again. Finally, in a shaky voice he stammered, "I didn't mean to shoot you. I didn't mean to do it."

The odor of the filthy bathroom and the man's sweaty body made Vicky's head spin dizzily. The room spiraled and spun as she drifted in and out of consciousness. Then Vicky realized someone else was in the room, too. A woman was exclaiming, "What have you done? Now what are we going to do?!"

Rana paused and ran her hand across her face.

"Don't stop now!" I demanded. "What *did* they do?"

"Threw her into her car, drove Vicky to the hospital, and left her there," Rana said. "It just so happened several policemen were there on another matter, so Vicky, finally feeling safe, told a police-woman the whole story as the doctors were working on her. But . . . get this! . . . no one believed her! At least not until the police went back to the warehouse and found her purse, a trail of blood, and a gun in the trash pail. Then they found the guy and arrested him."

Sad, sad story. But the ending had an even sadder twist. The attacker, who had three other convictions of attempted rape, was released after three years in jail. Vicky didn't get off so easily. She will spend the rest of her life in a wheelchair, completely paralyzed.

Rana shook her head thoughtfully. "It will be a real miracle if that woman ever smiles again."

A real miracle? All I could think of was that Vicky's story must not end there. Not if my dream to help other people had anything to do with it.

"I don't know how you disabled people do it," Rana continued. Then, with mild disgust she added, "And I sure don't know how you can believe in a God who would allow all this stuff."

I was silent. My thoughts shifted from Vicky to Rana. She was asking about one of the great mysteries of my faith. And it sure couldn't be handled in a trite or prepackaged way. Vicky's story would test the faith of the most steadfast of saints. Who could explain it? Yet I had asked for the chance to talk to real people in the real world, and now here it was.

"What we need is wisdom," I began hesitantly. "And wisdom is not the ability to figure out why God has done what He has done and what He'll do next."

"Then what is it?" Rana asked.

"It's trusting in Him even when nothing seems fair." Then I added, "You know, we can have faith that it's possible to doubt and still believe."

"So what's the big deal about God that He's worth that kind of trust?" Rana asked. In expressing her doubts, she seemed to actually be asking for understanding.

> It is to our benefit that we are not satisfied in a world destined for decay.

I grinned. I liked her honesty. "Look, Vicky's case is bad—no getting away from it. But far worse is *why* people shoot and rape and . . . whatever. In other words, sin. And not only the sin of crazy jerks like that man in the warehouse. I'm talking about you and me. We're sinners, too."

"Sin! Now there's something I know about," Rana said in mock pride. Then she told me *her* story. After her divorce, she went looking for good times with reckless abandon. What did it matter? She wasn't hurting anyone. After giving me more seamy details, she stopped and waited. For what, I'm not sure. Shock? Disgust? Astonishment? A lecture?

My expression didn't change. My own sin was a glaring reminder of the sorts of things I am actually capable of doing and being.

"Sin should never surprise us," I finally said. "I am really . . . really . . . no different . . . no better than you. The surprise is that God forgives any of us." Looking her straight in the eyes, I added, "And that, Rana, is the big deal about God."

"I don't think I understand," Rana said.

"Well, don't worry," I told her. "I think it'll all become clear."

I could not get Vicky out of my mind. Although I prayed and watched for an appropriate time to talk to her again, the opportunity just wasn't there.

Several days later when Rana and I were together, she again brought up the subject of God's forgiveness. As we talked, she described her own pain and disappointments. That afternoon, when she went home, she had a Bible in her hands with specific verses marked. The next afternoon she looked me up to tell me that she had prayed to acknowledge Jesus Christ as her Lord and Savior.

The thrill in Rana's voice and the new light in her smile were like a fresh wind that blew renewed strength and excitement into my soul.

My prayers had been for Vicky Olivas, yet God saw fit to bring Rana Leavell to Himself. How I rejoiced. Now there were two of us concerned for Vicky!

In my eagerness to help Vicky along, I jumped in with both feet. Rana and I took her to dinner, and I put my whole heart into the project of seeing Vicky come to the Lord. As Vicky left the restaurant, I smiled and thought, *That went pretty well, if I do say so myself.*

On the way home Rana said, "Look, Joni, I'm a novice at being a Christian, but . . . I don't know how to put this . . . but, you . . . well, you can't just waltz into her life with ready-made answers, no matter how much you want to help."

That really hurt.

Humbled, I realized that God had used a brand-new baby Christian to point an admonishing finger at me. I so wanted to do the right thing, to say the right thing, to use the perfect words to help Vicky. But I was embarrassed to realize that she had become less of a person and more of a project to me. I thought about formulas, plans, designs, programs, and organized efforts. Was this how God wanted Joni and Friends to proceed? Or was there a better way?

There was, and Rana helped me find it. We loved Vicky, Rana and I. We did things together, we went places together, and together we shared our ups and our downs. When it could be done without pushing, I spoke of Christ. Once in a while I gave Vicky a Scripture I felt would help. Rana and I prayed for her, and every now and then, when the moment seemed right, we told her we did.

One time Rana, Vicky, and I were together at a camp in Colorado when Vicky read Colossians 2:6–7 to us: "Just as you received Christ Jesus as Lord, continue to live in him, rooted and built up in him, strengthened in the faith as you were taught, and overflowing with thankfulness."

"I'm already weak—in every sense of the word," Vicky told us. "I have nowhere to go but up. It makes sense that I'll only get stronger if I put my faith in Christ."

And that is exactly what she did. The reality of the change was obvious in the way she devoured Scriptures and quickly grew in the Lord.

But one question continued to nag at her: Why should her attacker, three times convicted of attempted rape, be released after three years while she had to spend the rest of her life completely paralyzed in a wheelchair? As she flipped through the pages of her Bible with her mouthstick, she read verse after verse that sounded an awfully lot like pompous boasting from God—He's in charge for our good and His glory, so snap out of it and learn to "rejoice in suffering." And then, on top of that, she was admonished to forgive the one who had done her wrong! It was almost like rubbing salt into her open wound.

Rejoice? How? Forgive? It wasn't possible! Not when it was all so unfair. All she could pray was, "Lord, I will never walk again. I've got a leaky legbag . . . I smell like urine . . . my back aches. I'll never again be able to hug my son. Maybe You see all of this achieving some eternal glory, but all I see is one awful day after the next in this stinking wheelchair. It's not fair! Especially not now with that awful man out of jail and back on the streets!"

Our pain and sense of fairness always seem to scream, "Forget the future! What's God going to do to make things right *now?*" These demands tighten the screws on the moment, making us anxious to find quick fixes, escape hatches, or fair and just solutions. That's certainly what it was like for Vicky as she pitied her plight in her wheelchair. And the fact that her attacker escaped real justice only further weighted the scales against God.

But she kept reading. When she came to Romans 5:3 and read, "rejoice in our sufferings," her first thought was, *Sure, God, I'll rejoice the day You make things fair! And if You don't, then You tell me, what is going on? Are You trying to convince me I'm in spiritual denial? That hurt and pain are imaginary?*

Yet Vicky continued to study and pray, and God began to open her eyes to His perspective. That was the key, for perspective changes everything. And it is only by His hand that we come to where we are able to catch a glimpse of eternal perspective. You see, our human fairness is not meant to be balanced. It is to our benefit that we are not satisfied in a world destined for decay.

> *Fairness isn't the issue.*
>
> *God's justice is.*

The apostle Paul had this perspective when he said, "For our light and momentary troubles are achieving for us an eternal glory that far outweighs them all" (2 Cor. 4:17). And regarding his own experiences with injustice, he added, "I consider them rubbish" (Phil. 3:8). The apostle Peter also had this perspective when he wrote to Christian friends who were being flogged and beaten: "In this you greatly rejoice, though now for a little while you may have had to suffer grief in all kinds of trials" (1 Peter 1:6).

The eternal perspective separates what is transitory from what is lasting. What is transitory—such as injustice, unfairness, and pain—will not endure. But what is lasting—such as the eternal weight of glory accrued from that pain and from our willingness to forgive—will remain forever. Everything else . . . numbing heartache, deep disappointment, and blatant injustices . . . *everything else*, no matter how real it seems to us on earth, is treated as inconsequential. Earthly hardships are hardly worth noticing.

That's not to say that Vicky's sufferings—or yours or mine—are light in themselves. No, paralysis and pain and earthly injustice only *become* light in contrast to the far greater weight on the other side of the scale.

One day that scale of justice will not only balance, it will be weighted heavily—almost beyond comprehension—to our good and to God's glory. It will mean a new appreciation for His justice—not fairness, but justice. It will mean the final destruction of death, disease, and devilish men. It will mean the vindication of God's holy name and the restoration of all things under Christ.

And do you know what else this new perspective does? It leads to forgiveness. That's because we know that in the end justice will have its day. It will either doom a rapist dead in his transgressions or release that same man alive in the righteousness of Christ. If Vicky has her way, it will be the latter rather than the former. Why? Because now she understands that the value of a soul . . . anyone's soul . . . even the soul of the man who robbed her of a huge part of her life . . . far outweighs the inconvenience of an immobile body.

Whenever I have a tough day and need to be reminded of such things, I give my friend Vicky Olivas a call. She is the one who now often counsels me, reminding me, "Joni, fairness isn't the issue. God's justice is. One day He'll make it plain to us. In the meantime, we trust Him. And we pray . . . just like I pray for that man who attacked me."

Vicky's ability to forgive is amazing. Then again, she's got an amazing God.

Each one should use
whatever gift he has received
to serve others, faithfully
administering God's grace
in its various forms.

1 PETER 4:10

3

YET WILL I TRUST
HIM . . . AND SERVE

*S*hort and sprightly, with shining blonde hair and bright blue eyes, a winning smile, a sharp intellect, and a happy spirit. Beautiful inside and out. That's Camille Beckham. I first met Camille when she came to our office with a deaf friend—I watched her fingers fly as she interpreted for her friend during our conversation. More than an hour passed. I noticed something incredible. Camille's skill, concentration, and enthusiasm had not flagged one iota. This was a dedicated servant of Christ.

Where did Camille gain this huge affection for the Deaf population? It's not as though she considers herself

Camille Beckham

a missionary to the Deaf. No. She sees herself as an active part of the Deaf community. She enjoys the culture, loves the language, gets the jokes, and thoroughly enjoys hanging out with her friends who are Deaf. She has, in fact, been mistaken for being Deaf—by those who *are* Deaf.

It all began in the summer of 1982 when she was seventeen years old and in Haiti on a two-week mission trip with Youth for Christ. During the day her team worked hard sawing boards and pounding nails, carefully laying coats of blue and white paint on the schoolhouse and doing maintenance odds and ends. At night they attended church meetings where they took turns sharing their testimonies of what God had done in their lives. They bathed in the nearby river, slept in sleeping bags spread out on the concrete floors of the schoolhouse they were repairing, ate goat meat with the locals, and all got sick. And they loved it.

One evening the group walked to downtown St. Michel to get Cokes. Somehow, word spread among the under-twelve population, and suddenly the Americans were surrounded by curious Haitian kids eager to touch their white skin and feel their straight hair.

"Hi!" Camille said in her fractured Creole. With a big smile on her face, she shook one little black outstretched hand after another. "What's your name?" she asked each child in turn.

Most children responded eagerly and jostled for a chance to grab her hand. But one little boy was different. Oh, he shook her hand and smiled, all right, but he didn't respond to her question. Camille winked at him and said, "Don't you have a name?" He continued to smile, but he remained silent.

Another boy pushed his way past the silent boy and grabbed Camille's hand. As he pumped it energetically, he announced, "Hi! My name's Pierre. Him back there, that's just George. He can't talk and he can't hear . . . he's stupid."

Camille smiled at Pierre, but her attention was tugged back to George. Looking him straight in the eye, she smiled and shook his hand once more. *That little boy is going to know that I acknowledge him,* she determined. *He's going to understand that I see him as someone of great value.*

"Let's sing!" the children called out. Fortunately, the visiting students had learned some Christian songs in Creole, so right there in the downtown square, they led the children in singing.

I have joy in my soul!
I have joy in my soul!
I have joy in my soul to-day!

Little George couldn't sing, but when everyone clapped, Camille looked straight at him and distinctly clapped out the beat so that he would be able to clap along.

The next day, when Camille glanced out the window of the school where her team was working, she was amazed at what she saw. Just off the dusty road, little George was standing silently under a tree waiting for her. Camille ran outside, and although she didn't know a single word of sign language, she and the boy managed to communicate a bit through gestures.

I want a balloon, George gestured.

Camille pulled the empty pockets of her jeans inside out and shrugged her shoulders. *Sorry, no balloons.*

Then she got an idea—maybe George could read. When she gestured writing, he got very excited, so she ran to get a pad and pen. George took them, and to Camille's delight he wrote carefully and laboriously. But when Camille looked at George's "writing," her smile faded. It was nothing but a long series of straight little lines. It looked like writing, but it didn't mean a thing. Poor George. He so badly wanted to communicate, but he just didn't know how. Eight years' worth of ideas and feelings and experiences and emotions—a whole lifetime to him—were locked up inside, and he had no way of getting them out.

That fall, as a freshman at Stanford University, Camille was enthralled by her dorm mate's talk about the American Sign Language (ASL) course she was taking. "It's a completely different language from English," her friend explained. "It even has a different grammar. Some signs can't be translated exactly into English, and some English can't be translated exactly into signs. And you know what? Deaf people, even those right here in the United States, have their own distinct culture and values, history and jokes."

Camille was fascinated. With little George in mind, she enrolled in ASL. She was such an enthusiastic student that her instructor brought her along into the Deaf community and introduced her to many of her own Deaf friends. (Because Deaf communities function much more like cultural and language groups than disabled groups, Deaf Americans prefer to be referred to with a capital "D," just like Americans or Russians or Koreans.)

After a while, Camille felt comfortable enough to ask her new Deaf friends about their experiences with church and with God.

"God is really for hearing people," one young woman signed. "You know, there are lots of churches around, but they are all hearing churches. It's not really our thing."

When Camille offered that there was a church nearby with an interpreter, someone responded, "Does that mean God needs an interpreter to communicate with us?"

A young man signed, "Sure, I could go to that interpreted ministry, but then I would just be an object of someone else's ministry there. I could never be a teacher or leader or elder or anything in a hearing church."

A hearing church? As opposed to . . . ?

Of course! A church for the Deaf. Why not?

Following God's leading, Camille worked out a college major that let her study the Deaf community and language from many different perspectives with a good dose of personal experience mixed in. Then in 1984 she attended summer school at Gallaudet University in Washington, D.C.—the only Deaf university in the world.

In her senior year, Camille felt a strong call to do foreign mission work with Deaf people. But how? And when? And where? She had no idea. All she knew was that God had called her and it was all in His hands.

God used a Deaf person to put Camille in touch with us at Joni and Friends, and she served here as Deaf Ministry Coordinator for two and a half years. She left to enroll at Gallaudet University as a full-time grad student. Since 90 percent of the students there are Deaf, it was the closest thing to immersion in the Deaf language and culture she could find. Once again she saw great spiritual hunger . . . and a resigned sense that God was not for Deaf people.

Then came Vesta Sauter, founder and president of Deaf Opportunity Out Reach (DOOR). She had already been to Romania to minister to the Deaf. When she first arrived in Bucharest she had had a real problem. She knew Deaf people usually congregated in Deaf clubs or associations, but how could an American find those places? Bucharest was a huge city crowded with tall, plain gray buildings that all looked alike. Which one could possibly be the right one? No one seemed able to help her.

If God wants me to minister, Vesta thought, *He'll have to show me where to start.*

Then she got into a cab and set out along the streets and back roads looking for someone . . . anyone . . . anything . . . that might be a clue. As the cab passed an overgrown, trash-strewn city park, the taxi driver gestured toward a man standing on the corner— signing to another man! Almost before the driver could put on the brakes, Vesta was out of the cab and introducing herself. That very night the two men took her to a meeting at a Deaf club.

At the club, the leader signed to Vesta, "Tell us about yourself."

What an opening!

"I want to tell you about Jesus," Vesta signed in response. "He is far more than just the dead man on the cross you see in Orthodox churches." For several hours the group stood and watched her flying hands. "He is alive!" Her face beamed as she shared the good news of Christ. "And He wants a relationship with you. Yes, with you . . . the Deaf people."

When Vesta returned home, she asked Camille to come along on the next trip.

Vesta and Camille arrived in Romania with boxes and boxes of illustrated Romanian New Testaments. The next day they went back to the club with the boxes in tow. When the people saw there were Bibles in the boxes, they all rushed forward, shoving and struggling to grab a copy.

"Don't worry," Camille quickly signed. "There are plenty of Bibles for everyone." But that wasn't what experience had told them. After decades of lining up for bread and just about every other essential during the Communist regime, the Romanians couldn't believe there would be enough of anything.

I can just picture it—the great Deaf Bible Riot! People struggling and pushing their way to the front of the crowd. Some resorting to hitting, even kicking. Yanking on Vesta's and Camille's clothes in their efforts to grab Bibles out of their hands. It was a precious book . . . so precious that each person there was ready to fight to get a copy.

When Camille told me about that day, her sparkling blue eyes dimmed and her face clouded over. "I had a Bible of my own in my bag that day, and I had five others sitting at home on my bookshelf," she said. "When I saw their desperation to have a Bible, I was so convicted. Have I ever grasped my Bible as tightly as they did? Do I rush to open it and see what it has to say to me? Do I really, truly comprehend the incredible value of God's Word?"

She didn't answer her own questions. Neither did I. We take so much for granted.

The next week, Vesta and Camille announced that there would be a Deaf church meeting at the Holy Trinity Baptist Church. A church just for Deaf people? No one had ever heard of such a thing! One hundred fifty people showed up. Through stories, skits, and signed explanations, Vesta and her team presented the gospel while Camille prayed. Afterward they invited anyone who was interested in finding out more about what it means to know Christ personally to stand up. All 150 people stood.

Obviously they had misunderstood.

"Sit back down," the team signed. Again they explained that the invitation was only for those who were interested in more information about a personal relationship with Jesus. They paused. "If you aren't interested in more information, there is plenty of free Pepsi and lots of cookies outside waiting for you." The promise of free food—that would cull out any who weren't *really* interested.

Again, all 150 stood up.

Now, here was something they had never expected. There were only five workers there. Quickly they divided everyone into groups of about thirty. They assigned a worker to each group, and they went right on sharing. Many people came to know Christ that day!

Over the years, I have gleaned many lasting and powerful memories from ministry, but only a few matched the scene I witnessed the morning after I joined the group in Romania. I came down to the hotel restaurant, and there by the window sat Vesta and Camille at a long table with four or five new Deaf converts to Christ. These were men who, just that week, had first learned the name of Jesus—they knew the sign for God, but had asked in sign language, "Who is this Jesus you're telling me about?" When Vesta and Camille shared the good news, they had been among those who prayed to receive Christ.

Every single one of us is called to serve, whether you serve those with damaged bodies, damaged emotions, or injured spirits.

And there they were, like New Testament disciples, sitting with the two women who had given them the Living Water. Vesta and Camille knew they would be leaving within hours, and so, over an open Bible, they were covering as much doctrinal ground as humanly possible, explaining the virgin birth, the Resurrection, who Matthew, Mark, Luke, and John were, and where the Bible talked about heaven and hell. I sat behind the door, peering in, feeling as though I were with the apostle Paul in Corinth or with Barnabas in Asia Minor as I watched Vesta and Camille cram in as much as they could. And, oh, the sight of those Deaf men leaning forward with expressions of joy and expectation!

The next day Camille and Vesta went on to Cluj, where they had planned a similar evangelism outreach. They arrived at the meeting place forty-five minutes early so they could get set up before anyone else got there. But instead of the empty room they expected to find, there were fifteen Deaf people eagerly waiting for them. One woman rushed up to Camille and rapidly signed, "I've been praying for years that someone would come to tell us about Jesus. You are the answer to our prayers!" A man with white hair and a deeply lined face was right behind her. He had a tattered Bible under his arm. "Somewhere in here is the story of Noah," he signed. "Would you tell it to us? Please?"

Instead of setting up the room, Camille sat down and began to sign the story of Noah. When that story was finished, they asked for another one, then another, and another, right up until the time the program began.

How I would love to see such urgency to hear God's Word!

Oh, that I would have such fervor!

As the two women flew back to the States, Vesta talked about the future. The work in Romania was far from finished. They were leaving so many brand-new, undiscipled, Deaf Christians completely on their own. What would happen to them?

"So how about it?" Vesta said to Camille. "Would you be willing to coordinate trips back to Romania?"

She was. And she did such a good job that a few months later Vesta invited her to come to work for DOOR, coordinating their foreign mission work.

"Isn't God amazing?" Camille exclaimed when I talked to her. "He called me to serve the Deaf and He sent me, but He had so much preparation in mind for me in between! He knew just what I needed."

In the next several years, DOOR sent more than thirty short-term mission teams to Romania. As the teams worked with local believers, they saw five Deaf churches planted. But that's not all—the six hundred or so Christians in those Deaf churches have such a burden for the many, many Deaf Romanians who still don't know Jesus that they are now coordinating an outreach to the Deaf people in thirty-plus Romanian cities!

In January 2000, Camille moved to the beautiful city of Budapest, Hungary, as part of a DOOR mission team that includes an American couple with three children, a single American woman, and a Romanian couple. She is the only hearing person among them. In this wonderful city, with its mix of old and new, dilapidated and renovated, they established a European Deaf Christian training center. Their goal is to train Deaf church planters from Europe and the former Soviet Union in the unique ways of worship, singing, praying, and preaching in the "heart language" of the Deaf. Once trained, these people can go back to their homes and plant strong, reproducing Deaf churches.

One Sunday, they had an informal worship time with the Bulgarian students who had arrived early. One of the team members prayed—in sign language. Another signed a song in Romanian sign language. Yet another signed a song with the children.

A young woman named Senka was unable to hold in her joy. With hands flying she signed, "This is amazing! I mean, did you see what Nina and Laci and the others were doing? That was *Deaf* singing! Ever since I've been a Christian, I've seen hearing people singing, and I've watched an interpreter sign it, but I never really got it. I wanted to experience that same sense of God's presence the hearing people seemed to experience, but music through an interpreter never meant much to me. Will we learn how to sing like that? Please, please, will you teach us?"

Again God's call was clear. And today, that's exactly what they are doing. That lone missionary training center in Budapest set a vision to equip Deaf national believers to reach hundreds of thousands of people who are Deaf. Right now they have students from Romania, Moldova, and Bulgaria.

Bulgaria is a good example of the incredible job Camille and her small team are doing. Consider this: Although there are an estimated fifteen *thousand* Deaf people in Bulgaria, they could find only twenty-five Deaf Christians in the entire country. That's exactly why Camille is dedicated to training and raising up solid, committed Christian leaders in the Deaf community.

You say Camille's ministry is unique? You're right. So is mine. But, then, so is yours . . . whatever it is. You see, every single one of us is called to serve, and each one of us has a unique ministry in that we all touch different people. Whether you serve a big crowd of people, just a few, or only one. Whether you serve those with damaged bodies, damaged emotions, or injured spirits.

I received a Christmas card from Camille this year, and in it was a photo of her sitting in front of the bridge over the Danube River that divides the city of Budapest. She is as lovely as ever, and her eyes are still as bright, shining, and happy as always. I thought about the sacrifices Camille has made—she has invested so much of her life into missionary work that she's had no time to think about men, let alone marriage (she probably would say differently!).

I know for certain that Camille is thrilled with the life she has chosen. Years ago when she was spending time in my home, we "pajama partied" on my bed with popcorn and open Bibles. She said, "Joni, I simply want to empty myself entirely of every want or wish that might keep the Spirit of Christ from overflowing my life. I just want Jesus. I want to please Him and reach the people He loves. And I know that if I don't share the gospel with Deaf people, who will? Who will go?"

She flipped to Romans 10:14 and read, "'How, then, can they call on the one they have not believed in? And how can they believe in the one of whom they have not heard? And how can they hear without someone preaching to them?'"

I knew back then that Camille was one "called" young woman. What a moment. I knew I was looking into the open, eager face of a girl who would change the world for Christ. The world of those who cannot hear.

Thank God, Camille heard the call.

Thank God, she was willing to serve.

For everyone born of God

overcomes the world.

∽

1 JOHN 5:4

4

YET WILL I TRUST
HIM . . . AND OVERCOME

*I*f you know Jesus, you also know He loves
children. Red and yellow, black and white . . .
they are precious in His sight. It's easy to picture the
scene in Matthew 19:14–15 where Jesus says to His
disciples, "'Let the little children come to me, and do
not hinder them, for the kingdom of heaven belongs to
such as these." I can visualize the Lord tousling a little
boy's hair or bouncing a child on His knee. I can see
Him crouching to get to eye-level with a girl crying
because she feels left out . . . and I see Him giving her a
hug and a pat-pat on the back.

It Jesus had such enormous love for children who

could walk up to Him, how much more did His heart go out to children who couldn't walk?! He must be absolutely wild about kids who struggle with disabilities. His compassion must overflow for a little boy with muscular dystrophy or a little girl with cerebral palsy. A girl like Emily Shanahan.

I first met Emily—or Em, as I like to call her—when I wheeled into the meeting room at our Joni and Friends Family Retreat at Oakwood Inn, Indiana. She was the cutest thing on wheels, sitting in her small pink wheelchair. I took one look at this nine-year-old, her big brown eyes, that smiling face, and her hair done up in bouncy pigtails with pink ribbons, and I melted. I was especially glad that when we broke up into small prayer groups, Emily Shanahan parked her wheelchair next to mine.

Emily Shanahan and me

When it came her turn to pray, I couldn't help but peek. Her small body may have been stiff and rigid with cerebral palsy, but her head gracefully bowed as she prayed softly and eloquently. Emily's cerebral palsy has affected her speech somewhat, and so I tried very hard to listen closely.

"Dear God, thank You for dying on the cross for us and thank You for my mom and dad who love me very much and who take such good care of me—"

I could hardly believe my ears. *This nine-year-old knows about prayer. She really knows Jesus!*

"—and I want to ask You to please help my parents and bless them because they love You and I love them very much, too, and please help me to be a good daughter and thank You that my parents can come to this retreat to relax and—" Emily's pigtails bobbed as she breathed in between the spaces of her long sentence. "—it's so neat that my parents get to have time off from taking care of me here at Retreat and so I thank You for the volunteer who's helping me, and I love You, Jesus, and bless all the other kids here at the retreat, too."

Others in our prayer group—myself included—prayed after little Em, but I sensed that Jesus was still lingering over her words. I've always thought that the prayers of children possess a particular power with God; that day I felt it.

Emily Shanahan and I became fast friends at that retreat. My affection for this little girl only deepened long after the camp ended. As the seasons flew by, I kept abreast of her adventures, including the new surgeries on her legs and hips. Time and again,

I was encouraged when I read her E-mail reports: "I'm doing fine, Joni. Thanks to Jesus!" I could just picture her smile and pigtails bobbing as she plunked the computer keys with her finger.

Em is twelve years old now, but she hasn't lost an ounce of spunk and sparkle, despite her occasional physical setbacks. Recently I took the liberty of recording one of our "talks" together because I want you to know this special girl as I do. I should explain that Emily Shanahan was born twelve weeks premature on a warm summer day in August of 1988 in Dayton, Ohio. Although she cannot walk due to her cerebral palsy, she can drive her pink power wheelchair and can also use a stander that helps stretch her muscles. With an adaptive fork, Em is able to feed herself a little bit. She has had four major surgeries and has, twice, lain for months in a body cast. I asked Emily, "What has been your toughest circumstance to overcome?" and this is what she said:

"One of the struggles I had to overcome when I was in kindergarten was that my parents didn't know that I could be in regular classes, so they put me in a Multiple Handicapped (MH) classroom. MH school started two weeks after regular school did. So I went to regular school for two weeks. Then, when MH school started, I spent part of the day in kindergarten and part of the day in the MH class, which I was supposed to do for the rest of the year. I hated it! So on the second day they tried to move me from the regular kindergarten class to the MH class. I turned my chair off in the middle of the hallway when I realized what they were doing."

Emily and me at a dress-up occasion at Joni and Friends family camp

Stop and picture that. That kindergartner had chutzpah. Can you imagine the teachers on either side of Em's wheelchair, escorting her down the hallway when—*bam!*—suddenly the chair died. They probably thought her batteries gave out! But not so. Em continued . . .

"At that time I had a toggle switch, so I covered the toggle switch with my hand and said that I wasn't going anywhere. They didn't know what to do. You see, I had just gotten my chair, and they didn't know they could disengage the motors and push me down the hall. Well, to make a long story short, the school had to call my mom and say I wouldn't have to go to the MH class but she would have to come and get me. Mom and Dad ended up having a meeting with the school, and they decided that I could be there at the regular classroom. It's been that way ever since then. I've gotten straight A's in the last quarter of fifth grade, and I hope I continue in that from now on. I was getting A's and B's before."

I bet the teachers thought they had a problem child on their hands, but Emily Shanahan isn't militant or aggressive and, no, she would never chain her wheelchair to a regular classroom in protest or carry a "Teachers Unfair!" poster down the hallway. (Then again, maybe she would.) Rather, Emily is just plain assertive. In a nice way. And *that's* what won over her teachers.

It was at that Family Retreat when I noticed that Emily was very good at making friends. I wondered if it had always been that way. When I asked, she said, "When I was in third grade, I told my mom that I wanted to have an overnighter. My mom said that it would be okay and what friend did I want to have over? I told her that I wanted to have an overnighter at someone else's home other than ours! I saw the look on my mom's face that said, 'That is something I can't give you.' At that time, we committed my desire to prayer and claimed Matthew 19:26: 'With man this is impossible, but with God all things are possible.'

"One month later, my mom went to a weekend Women's Retreat. She shared a hotel room with four other women, one of whom was Julie Martin. While they were getting ready for bed one night, Julie told my mother that she and her husband, Jon, had been thinking of inviting me, Emily, for an overnighter at their home. You see, they have a daughter Christi who is my age! Mom and Julie began to cry as my mom shared my prayer request from weeks before. I have not only had one overnighter in their home, but three! I even get to use my power wheelchair in their home!"

Wow. I looked into Em's liquid brown eyes and thought about all the times she had held disappointment at bay. Disappointment at not being able to run on strong legs to the school playground. At not being able to play dodgeball like the rest of the kids at recess. And disappointment that, at least up to that point, no one had ever offered, "Hey, Emily, how about bringing your sleeping bag over to my house this weekend?!" I also thought about the equal number of times Emily probably took those disappointments to God in prayer. The result? What seemed impossible was now possible. This overcomer now has a stronger heart, a deeper faith, and a lot of overnighters at the homes of new friends.

As I came to know Emily better and as I watched her interact with other children at the Family Retreat, it occurred to me that this kid was out to change the world. Not just her world, *the* world. Case in point:

"In the spring of my fourth-grade school year, my class was going on a field trip to the Ohio Caverns. I couldn't help but think of Isaiah 55:8–9, "'For my thoughts are not your thoughts, neither are your ways my ways,' declares the LORD. "As the heavens are higher than the earth, so are my ways higher than your ways and my thoughts **than** your thoughts.'" From an earthly standpoint, I was limited in what I could do on this field trip, but once committed to God, His plans were revealed!

"My teacher wanted me to go on the trip but said that I would pretty much have to stay in the gift shop while my classmates went down into the cave. My mom began to pray about adaptive ideas for my involvement in this field trip to the Ohio Caverns. About three days later, God gave my mom the idea to write the local Fire Department and ask them to do a practice cave rescue with me down into the cave entrance while strapped into a gurney. Once down in the cave, they could prop me up against a wall to take in the sights of the cave. (My mom did ask me if I was okay with this idea before she wrote the letter. I said, 'Yes.')

"After writing the letter, my mom got a call from the local fire chief and he stated that he could not take me down into the entrance of the cave, so Mom said, 'Well, that's okay' and began to hang up. He said, 'Mrs. Shanahan, wait! My emergency personnel can take Emily down the exit instead!' My mom said, 'I understand there are sixty-six steps down the exit versus thirty-four steps in the entrance of the cave!' He said, 'Ma'am, we are here to serve the community!'

"I had to go down the exit since all my classmates would be going down the entrance and I would block their entry into the Caverns. Once I got to the Ohio Caverns, the paramedics transferred me from my wheelchair and onto the gurney. They even had special padding for my legs and a blanket to keep me warm, and I had my own tour guide. I was never propped up against the wall to take in the sights of the cave. I was carried through almost all of the cave by the paramedics. One lady paramedic had the sole job of making sure my face never got hit by a stalactite!

"We came to one point where I could no longer fit through the rocks while in the gurney. So two paramedics took me out and carried me in their arms to see the highlight of the cave, called the Stalactite King, then carried me back to the gurney and strapped me back in to begin the exit trip out of the cave and back up sixty-six steps! Once transferred back into my power wheelchair, my classmates began to come out of the exit and I joined them for lunch.

"I am reminded of Mark 2:1–5 where the paralytic was lowered into the roof by four of his friends after they dug a hole in the roof so the paralytic could ask Jesus for forgiveness of his sins. I am thankful for my friends who demonstrate that type of selfless love to me on a daily basis so that my life is full and complete, filled with grace because of God's love for me."

Can you see why I'm in love with the divine Miss Em? Talk about overcoming the odds! And I am humbled to report that Emily loves me. Am *I* the blessed one, or what! When I asked how my wheelchair has helped her, she told me this:

"I think the most important thing in life is for us to have a personal relationship with Jesus Christ so that people can go to heaven and have a party with all their friends instead of being in turmoil down in hell. I believe this because the day after my fifth birthday party I felt there was no purpose for my life. I began to cry and told my mom that my legs were only cute ornaments to put tights on. My mother tried to comfort me, but I didn't want to hear anything about God.

"Three days later, Joni, I was listening to your *Harps & Halos*

CD that Mom ordered a few weeks prior to this ache I felt in my heart. Mom was doing the dishes, and I heard your words to the song 'Gonna Go to Heaven,' and a peace came over me. You sang:

Some people think they'll spend forever pushing up the grass.
But I believe I have a date to leave this earth at last.
That graveyard is just a place to hang this old suit to dry.
And with a brand-new body I will spread my wings and fly.[1]

"My mom thought the words were inappropriate and she started to turn it off. But then she noticed my peacefulness. From that point on, Ephesians 1:11 became very real to me. It says in *The Living Bible*, 'Moreover, because of what Christ has done we have become gifts to God that he delights in, for as part of God's sovereign plan we were chosen from the beginning to be his, and all things happen just as he decided long ago.' I realize I've been chosen and God is going to do something special with my life. I have the hope of eternal life, and I can give that message to others I encounter. My handicapped body is only temporary and can be used by God to touch others' lives while I am here on earth."

I'll say it again. Jesus loves the little children, all the children of the world. Red and yellow, black and white, lame and deaf and without sight. Jesus loves *all* the children of the world. Children like Emily Shanahan. And may I share Em's words of advice to other kids?

"The message I want to give to other kids is, and I know this sounds strange because this is a kid writing this, but be thankful for your parents. They do a lot for you. They help you with your homework. They help you make big decisions. And think about it: you wouldn't be able to get together with your friends most of the time, if it weren't for them. I am especially thankful for my mom and dad because they have to do a lot of other stuff for me, such as brushing my teeth, giving me a shower, getting me dressed."

How grateful to God I am for her parents, Tom and Barb, who have prayed and worked hard to build up their child's faith. Their daughter is a life-picture of Isaiah 11:6, for "a little child shall lead them." Tom and Barb have taught her to be an overcomer, and maybe that's why Em's favorite Scripture is Jeremiah 29:11: "'For I know the plans I have for you,' declares the LORD, 'plans to prosper you and not to harm you, plans to give you hope and a future.'"

Emily's hope for her future is a growing and vibrant friendship with Jesus Christ. He positively affects everything she says and does. And I believe the cerebral palsy has been the tool He has used to hone and shape her noble, courageous little character.

It's a good thing. She'll need all the courage she can muster in the years to come. After Tom and Barb get older, and as Emily's preteen years give way to adulthood, others will give her the daily care she can't give herself. It won't be easy—I know that

> *"My handicapped body is only temporary and can be used by God to touch others' lives while I am here on earth."*

from personal experience. To wake up and wait for someone to bathe me, to dress me, to lift me into my wheelchair. To brush my hair and my teeth. Even after going through the routine countless times, I sometimes feel I just don't have the strength to face it one more day. And other people with less empathy will review her college entrance exams or job applications. Happy— yet sometimes hard—childhood days will give way to happy and *much* harder days of testing and disappointment. Somehow I'm not concerned for Emily, though. She's learned early how to be more than a conqueror—a lesson every one of us must learn sooner or later, whether we're disabled or able-bodied.

As for Emily, she is trusting God. And by His grace, she *will* overcome.

*Many are the plans
in a man's heart,
but it is the LORD's
purpose that prevails.*

PROVERBS 19:21

5

YET WILL I TRUST
HIM . . . AND BELIEVE

I was sequestered away behind a closed door, glued to my computer, when suddenly my co-worker Judy Butler came bursting into my office waving a copy of *USA Today.* "Look at what I just read. We can win this! I know we can!"

"Win what?" I said without looking up.

"It's the 'Bridge the World' contest sponsored by KLM Airlines, celebrating their seventy-fifth anniversary, and all we have to do is write a 750-word essay telling how we would use twenty-five free airline tickets and all the cargo space we need to fly to anywhere in the world to accomplish something that would 'bridge the world' of differences between people."

As Judy paused to take a breath, I turned to take a look at the full-page ad in the newspaper. Silently, we read all about the contest details and deadlines. After we finished, we whispered simultaneously, "We *can* win this."

We grabbed John Wern, director of "Wheels for the World," from the hallway to show him the ad. Wheels for the World is a program of Joni and Friends in which we collect used wheelchairs, refurbish them in prisons around the country, and then recruit teams of Christian physical therapists to travel with us overseas not only to fit the wheelchairs to needy disabled children and

Willie Doe Agbeti

adults, but also to give them Bibles and do disability ministry training in local churches. "John," I said, "I could easily write about how our ministry bridges the world of disability differences between disabled people around the world. Surely you could use twenty-five free tickets to go anywhere in the world with wheel-chairs and Bibles. What country should I write about?"

John rubbed his chin. A smile spread slowly across his face. "I know just the place," he said. John proceeded to explain how, ear-lier in the year, he and Wheels for the World had been in Ghana, West Africa, distributing wheelchairs and Bibles. The team had traveled 260 kilometers north of the capital city of Accra to reach the town of Kumasi, in the Ashanti region. It hadn't been easy. The dirt roads were rutted. Civil war was raging just north of the town, and it had been a dangerous journey. But our good African friend and sponsor, Willie Doe Agbeti, had told us that the needs among the poverty-stricken disabled people in that region were desperate.

"Many more people showed up that day at the wheelchair dis-tribution than we had wheelchairs for. Mothers had walked miles, carrying their disabled children in slings on their backs. It broke my heart to tell them we had no more chairs," John said, his eyes filling with tears. "But in the face of so much disappointment, those African women were so hopeful. They said to me, 'We know you'll come back. We know you'll return with more wheelchairs.'"

"So what did you say?" I asked.

"I promised them we'd come back."

"But, another trip to Africa isn't in your budget. All of those fam-ilies will be disappointed and ⸻ " I stopped. The three of us looked at one another and with hardly a word, we prayed, I turned back to my computer, and I began writing our essay. I asked the KLM contest committee to award Wheels for the World the free tickets and cargo space so we could return to Kumasi in Ghana, West Africa.

> Dear Friends at KLM . . . People with disabilities here in the U.S. have so much; some of us, even *two* wheelchairs. Yet there are needy individuals living in Africa who survive on the street and crawl in the dirt for lack of a wheelchair. Would you please help us bridge the gaping chasm between people like me, here . . . and friends over there?! A gift of twenty-five tickets and cargo space will enable us to make a huge difference in their lives!

The essay was soon completed and we mailed everything off to the KLM headquarters in Amsterdam, Holland.

Two days later, my husband, Ken, and Judy and I boarded a KLM plane to head to Budapest, Hungary, where Joni and Friends was holding a conference for disability leaders in Eastern Europe. As we exited the plane and wheeled through the Amsterdam airport, we saw "Bridge the World" contest posters *everywhere*. I smiled slyly at Ken after we passed the seventh poster and said, "See that? We're going to win it."

"Yeah, sure," he scoffed, "and I'm with the Prize Patrol from Publisher's Clearing House Sweepstakes."

Judy and I remained undaunted; John Wern, too. We tried to convince other coworkers that we were in the running to win, but

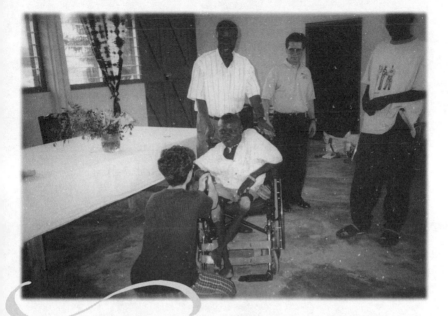

Willie and one of his friends who is being fitted for a wheelchair

it wasn't easy. One or two staff people even said, "Isn't what you did a little like gambling?" *Gambling? Is entering a contest considered wrong for a Christian?* No, my conscience wasn't troubled, but I did respect their point of view. Anyway, before my mind had a chance to make much of it, we received a call from Amsterdam. Praise God, we had won the contest! I almost jumped out of my wheelchair! Out of fifteen thousand entries from around the world, we—and eleven others—were chosen as grand prize winners. It may have been a gamble to some, but we were now free to start sketching plans to return to Africa.

Five months later, twenty-five of us arrived in Amsterdam where we were greeted and congratulated by KLM executives bearing gifts, T-shirts, and free cameras for our trip. Within a couple of hours we were off to Africa in a KLM 747 loaded with wheelchairs and other adaptive equipment for blind and mentally handicapped people. As we flew south over the Sahara Desert, I kept thinking about the families in the little town of Kumasi. I thought about the photos I had seen of the heart-wrenching poverty. I also kept thinking about Willie Doe Agbeti, who was helping us arrange this exciting trip to his country. I couldn't think of a finer, more *believing* Christian to work with in Africa than this dear gentleman.

Of course, back then my friendship with Willie was still new. I hadn't realized that ever since 1976 God had been preparing us both to minister to hurting people. Back in the seventies when I was asking God to show me a way He could use me, Willie Doe Agbeti was in West Africa doing the same. I was living in a middle-class suburban neighborhood in America; Willie was a struggling graduate student of Journalism wanting very much to show the love of God to the needy people in his home country of Ghana.

He got that chance when he moved to a new neighborhood—Osu, a suburb of the Ghanaian capital city, Accra. Suddenly he came face-to-face with an aspect of life totally new to him. A ragged neighborhood boy, crippled by polio, crawled past his apartment on all fours. Day after day Willie watched the young boy inching his way along the rock-strewn dirt road. Even when rain turned the road to a river of mud, he crawled by.

Who was this boy? Asking around, Willie learned that the boy's father—a medical doctor—had disowned him, and that his mother was completely overburdened by the tragedy that had struck her family. There was no government help available, and his neighbors cared nothing about him. Completely ostracized, he had been tossed out to languish on the fringes of society. That meant a life of loneliness, hopelessness, and crushing poverty.

Willie was shocked by the sight of the boy struggling along on thickly calloused knees and hands protected only by thin rubber sandals. But whenever he insisted, "We've *got* to do something," his suggestion was met by disinterested shrugs. He was so disturbed he couldn't sleep at night. When he did manage to doze off, he was plagued by nightmares about the boy with shriveled legs who crawled past his window.

Looking back on that time, Willie told me, "Deep within me I knew I could not leave that young man alone. It just would not be right."

Willie did his best to help the boy. He encouraged him to stay in school and walked with him every day. When heavy rain made the road impassable, he put the boy in a taxi and paid the fare. But Willie knew that even finishing school would not make a disabled boy like this employable. When Willie talked

Though the two of us were separated by every barrier known to man, we were already united in the mind of God.

to him about what he might want to do to support himself, the boy said he would like to be an accounts clerk. So Willie went to work scouting libraries for a foreign organization that would be willing to help the boy—by now a young man—achieve his goal. He was able to go to England for training, but when he came back he still couldn't find a job.

Sounds pretty discouraging, doesn't it? Not much of a start on a helping ministry.

But Willie never stopped believing he was doing what God wanted him to do. And a strange thing happened. Disabled people from all over the area began to descend on Willie's small apartment. From early morning until late at night they came, pleading with him for help.

Willie was overwhelmed. He had nothing to give them—no money, no office to meet in and listen to their stories, no place to refer them. "My room could take only a bed and two visitors at a time. And here I was with tens and tens of disabled people seeking help from me." But instead of helplessly wringing his hands . . . or locking his door! . . . Willie fell to his knees before God, the source of his faith and the provider of his needs.

"God, I need Your help!" Willie cried. "I can do nothing in this situation. I am trusting in You, Lord, to show me what to do."

But God was silent. Yet Willie trusted Him—and believed.

Still, with or without money, Willie was resolved to help this community of people. It was the right thing to do, both for the people themselves and to honor the God in whom he believed and placed his trust. "You may call it love," Willie explained. "You may call it compassion. But to me, it was my very being. I *had* to do it."

That very first young man Willie helped went to work as the

liaison between Willie and the other disabled people. He also brought in another disabled young man who became Willie's organizer, going from house to house with messages for the disabled. Together they formed the Disabled Talents Society to help the disabled help themselves. But they had no meeting place and no money to rent one. Even when Willie dug deep into his own pockets to rent a place, many disabled people couldn't come. They couldn't walk and they had no wheelchairs. So the society fell apart.

Still Willie believed.

The next year, as he completed his journalism training, he got an idea. Why not start a newsletter for the disabled? He could collect information on resource organizations and publish it along with directions for applying for assistance.

For six years Willie kept the newsletter going, and to a degree it was successful. But people still kept flocking to him for help. Now they were coming from as far away as Nigeria and the Ivory Coast! But what did he have to give them?

"I was wading into deeper waters. Again and again I went down on my knees and prayed, 'God, I need You more than ever! What do You want me to do?'"

But still he could discern no answer. Yet Willie trusted God— and believed.

That's not to say there was no help at all. The information services project of the United Nations did offer support . . . though not in the form of money. They sent materials. Lots and lots of it. More than Willie could possibly stuff into his small room. And all the UN was asking of Willie was that he distribute the material throughout all of West Africa! This had to be from God, he reasoned, but *how* was he to accomplish such a task!?

"God," Willie prayed frantically, "are You there?"

I'm not at all sure what I would do if I were in that position. I'm afraid I might send all those people home and go back to my journalism. But not Willie. He borrowed money and hired a taxi to haul reading material to the homes of six of his friends who had agreed to store as much as they could under their beds. That taxi traveled back and forth four times before it finished unloading the literature. When no more could be stuffed under his friends' beds, the rest was piled in Willie's room. "For several weeks, I just slept in the middle of all the brochures."

In the face of tempting alternatives, shortcuts, and quick-fix solutions, will you and I believe?

Willie wrote a letter to the UN saying, "Thanks, guys, for all the help. But please, no more materials!"

Yes, Willie was frustrated . . . and yes, he was overwhelmed. But he was a man of great faith. Because he was certain God wanted him to minister to the disabled, he never doubted that God would enable him to do it. The only questions were *how* and *when*.

"Finally I started turning my attention toward what I should have been doing in the first place. I looked toward local churches." He started by holding weekly Bible studies for disabled people. Then he rented vehicles to take them to church on Sundays. He went right to their houses and picked them up for church, then he brought them back home afterward. They loved it!

In 1990, Willie recruited three pastors and a few friends from different churches to begin developing special ministries for the disabled in the churches. They called it OMNIBILITY. On the day it was launched, Willie invited the press to attend. They came and listened attentively as he laid out his grandiose plans for the disabled all over Ghana.

"My plans were so high-flying that everyone was impressed."

But then one of the pressmen asked, "Sir, your plans seem to present a very good solution to the plight of the disabled in this society. But, sir, how are you going to finance it all?"

Willie was speechless. He had been too busy planning to think about such mundane details as money. But then, with complete conviction, he said, "God will provide."

The press didn't carry one single sentence on the launch or the plans.

Still, Willie had no doubt that he was doing what God wanted him to do. Still, he believed. He wasn't doing it for himself . . . he wasn't even doing it for disabled people . . . and he certainly wasn't doing it to bring riches or glory to himself. No, he was doing it for the glory of the Lord. Why, then, couldn't he see any direction from God?

And then God spoke.

One evening Willie wandered into a Christian bookstore and there he saw a copy of my book, *All of God's Children: How to Minister to Persons with Disabilities*

"I could not believe my eyes!" Willie told me. "The very thing I needed most in my life and for my ministry was mysteriously there in my hands! God had finally answered my prayers."

He opened the book and started reading. "Right there in the store, on my feet, I chewed every single letter and word in that book and gulped it down. I would have finished reading the entire book if the shopkeeper had not tapped me on the shoulder to say she was closing. I was that engrossed."

Willie paid for the book and took it home, and by midnight he had finished reading it. By dawn he had completed a letter to me. And you can believe I answered that letter the very day I received it. "William," I wrote, "where have you been all these years?"

The hand of God had brought us together. Though neither of us could have seen it, this was the very thing both of us had been praying for. Oh, the truth of Proverbs 19:21: "Many are the plans in a man's heart [and a woman's too!], but it is the LORD's purpose that prevails."

And that's exactly how it happened. God knew, and His plans did prevail. Just as they always do. In every situation and in every place all around the world.

And here God's plan was to finally allow Willie, an African, and me, an American, to come face-to-face through the Dutch KLM contest.

While our plane taxied at the Accra airport, I took in the surrounding area. The edges of the old runway were crumbling, weeds sprouted from cracks, and the small terminal looked a little run-down. When we parked on the tarmac, I noticed there weren't jetways. A couple of Africans in street clothes rolled the stairs to the jet door. When we exited, I took a deep breath of hot, wet air. The trees surrounding the airport were thick and dark green, and I could hear clapping, laughter, and music on the other side of the terminal. We were in West Africa—and was I excited!

While the wheelchairs and supplies were being unloaded, we settled in at the hotel near the airport. I could hardly sleep that night, thinking about the amazing circumstances that had brought us here. I lay awake, praying, *Lord, thank You for honoring the hopes of those women in Kumasi who got John to promise he'd return with more wheelchairs. Just a few months ago, it seemed an impossibility. But, here we are! And thank You for Your servant Willie Doe Agbeti who is preparing for our arrival. It's all because of You, Lord Jesus, and an incredible contest. Who would have believed it?!*

The next morning after breakfast, our twenty-five Wheels for the World team members—including physical therapists, special education teachers, friends of our ministry, and wheelchair mechanics—all gathered in a conference room in the hotel. It was time for orientation, after which we would separate into small groups to cover the cities of Accra, Tema, and Kumasi.

John Wern led the group in prayer and then turned the meeting over to Willie Doe Agbeti so he could explain the details and answer questions. However, before Willie began, he paused and reached for a piece of paper on the table. Quietly, he held it in both hands, as though he were about to read several notes. But he said nothing. Instead, his eyes became full and wet.

Finally, he broke the silence and said, "Some of you may not know this, but our capital city is the KLM hub for the continent of Africa. You also know that it is by the graciousness of God through this contest that we are able to gather here today. However, there is something you do not know." He hesitated, as if unsure, but then wiped his eyes and continued.

"Last year I, too, saw a newspaper advertisement for this contest. I had always had such great hopes for our outreach to disabled people in this country because . . . the needs are so desperate. I thought I would enter the contest to win a prize that would make money for our work, and so I began to write my essay. Yet as you can see"—at this point, Willie held up the paper by his thumb and forefinger—"I did not finish."

I squinted and saw that the paper was only half-filled with writing.

"I did not complete my essay because I felt God telling me it was gambling. I wanted very much to enter the contest, and so I kept asking, 'Lord, are You sure?' but I kept hearing Him saying, 'No, Willie, this is gambling. This is something you should not do.'" All of us were stunned. We sat still and waited for him to finish.

"God told me that if I obeyed Him, He would fulfill my deepest dreams. He would honor my desire to reach the disabled people in my country with His gospel. I scratched my head and wondered how God might do such an extraordinary thing . . . especially since He told me that I wasn't to enter the contest. But He said to me, 'Willie, just *believe.*' And now"—he spread his arms wide, as if to take us all in—"*now* look what God has done!"

The Lord would not permit Willie to enter the contest for the sake of his beliefs. Yet the Lord permitted me to enter the same contest and encouraged me to believe. And both of us experienced God's blessing.

I grinned and thought of Romans 14:3–4: "Those who think it is all right to eat such meat must not look down on those who won't. And if you are one of those who won't, don't find fault with those who do. For God has accepted them to be his children. They are God's servants, not yours. They are responsible to him, not to you. Let him tell them whether they are right or wrong. And God is able to make them do as they should" (TLB).

I've never met anyone who *believed* quite like William Doe Agbeti. I learned from Willie that a thing like a half-million dollars worth of airplane tickets and cargo means nothing to God. What *is* worth a half-million dollars is that Willie believed for more; and the Lord gave more than all of us, including Mr. Agbeti, could possibly ask or imagine.

In the face of tempting alternatives, shortcuts, and quick-fix solutions, will you and I believe? Will we say no to a compromise with our conscience, and yes to waiting on Him? Will we trust that God has a better idea? If we do, it will mean a richer, deeper life and ministry, and a rock-solid, unshakable confidence in the Lord.

As Willie would say, "Trust Him and believe,"

God has said,
"Never will I leave you;
never will I forsake you."

HEBREWS 13:5B

YET WILL I TRUST
HIM . . . EVEN THROUGH
QUESTIONS AND DOUBTS

The night was a starry dome above the Israeli kibbutz. Such a clear and cool evening made the sundown beginning of the Sabbath especially restful and quiet. It had been a long day of labor in the avocado fields, and Barbara Carey and her friends were relaxing and cooking *shukshuga,* a kind of Jewish fondue of mushrooms and cheese. The air was heavy with the spicy aroma of the food mixed with the sweet fragrance of wildflowers, and the mood was peaceful and serious. Barbara and her friends sat on the floor spreading the fondue on kibbutz bread. As the girls licked their fingers and sipped their kibbutz ration tea sweetened with honey, they talked about the day's labor in the fields.

Barbara Kolar kneeling beside me with her sisters Marilyn and Nancee

The months had been filled with one adventure after the next: visiting sheiks in their black tents staked near Beersheva. Bargaining with women in the marketplace. Making friends with Bedouins herding goats and camels. Meeting soldiers near Masada. Walking through the narrow, winding passages of Old Jerusalem, jostling with Arabs, passing women in long black dresses, and ducking in and out of countless little shops. And striking up conversations at crossroads with other bohemian backpacker types who were also out to see the world and taste something of romance and adventure.

Barbara sighed deeply and, with stomach full, leaned back on an overstuffed pillow. As she gazed into the fire, she thought, *Lord, I have loved being in Your land. Seeing where You walked, getting to know the people You loved. I want to know more about You and Your world.*

The campus of UCLA seemed a world away.

And it almost was. Barbara Carey's journey had begun several years before in 1958 when she was an art major at the university. After graduation, she was planning to study in Paris, to paint and travel, and to get to know the world outside America. Her plans took a detour when, during her first year on campus, a fellow student invited her to the college group at Hollywood Presbyterian Church. From there, Barbara got connected with the UCLA chapter of Campus Crusade for Christ. A CCC staff woman asked, "Barbara, have you ever read the Bible?" Barbara explained that she had tried, but she hadn't really succeeded in getting into it. The two of them began to meet, and within a short time the nineteen-year-old UCLA art major gave her life to Jesus Christ.

Barbara's school years had been a time of rapid growth. She dived into the discipleship program, memorizing Scriptures and learning how to share the gospel with foreign students. One could easily feel lost on the sprawling UCLA campus, but she held tightly to Hebrews 13:5: "For he hath said, I will never leave thee, nor forsake thee" (KJV). She had memorized John, chapters 14–17, which reminded her that Christ loved her, that He would never leave her, that He had given His Holy Spirit to comfort and to guide her, and that one day He would return to take her home. Barbara determined that she would love and obey Him and that she would bear fruit for the kingdom. In fact, this had become her single passion.

She had graduated, taught two years, saved up, and with her friend Cathie, decided to throw on a backpack and head to Israel to see the land of the Bible. Having interacted with Jewish students back at UCLA and attended several Jews for Jesus meetings, Barbara felt a passion to immerse herself in the culture of Israel. And so she and Cathie had signed on as volunteers at a kibbutz not far from Nazareth. Now that she was a Christian, it made sense to experience firsthand the roots of her new faith. For the past three months, she and Cathie had lived at the kibbutz, picking avocados, bananas, and grapes during the day, and at night, folk dancing with the Israelis.

Yes, Barbara thought, *I'm at home here.*

Barbara took her bread and wiped the last of the *shukshuga* from the bottom of the pot. Someone opened up a huge map of the world and spread it out on the table. Barbara leaned forward and let her eyes wander over the section of the Middle East: Turkey, Iran, Afghanistan, and Pakistan. All places filled with adventure possibilities.

Then someone pointed to India.

"I know a woman there!" Barbara exclaimed. "I met her at UCLA. I'd love to see her again."

There was so much Barbara longed to see, so many adventures she wanted to experience, so many people she hoped to meet. India was as good a place to continue her carefree life as anywhere. That night, the young women shook on it; India would be the next stop.

God Himself is the answer to all questions.

In early 1963 Barbara and Cathie boarded a ship in Haifa that took them to Istanbul. There in Turkey, Barbara wandered through the streets, mesmerized by the rich history and art all around her, the mosques and great marketplaces that harkened back to ancient times. With their Bibles within easy reach on top of their backpacks, they hitchhiked across Turkey and picked up a few phrases of Farsi in Iran. They met shepherds in Afghanistan, farmers in Pakistan, and in every city, students and foreigners who worked there. And they never missed an opportunity to say, "We are Christians. God is with us. He loves you." All the while, in lands so far away from home, she remembered the comforting words of Jesus: "I will never leave you nor forsake you." His Holy Spirit would comfort and guide

Finally they arrived in India. While living with a Hindu family, Barbara noticed that the woman would rise early to prepare special foods. One morning Barbara asked, "Who are you making food for?"

The Hindu woman did not look up but continued to chop the persimmons into quarters. "I am making offerings for the gods," she said.

Oh Lord, the young American silently prayed, *the world is full of so many hurting people. I'm just one person. Is there anything I can do to make a difference?*

Later that day in the marketplace, Barbara noticed women sewing flower garlands. She thought their work was fascinating and very lovely . . . until she peered into a temple to see people offering these same garlands to strange gods. Idols that were half man and half elephant. They all had bowls of food in front of them and many garlands piled around their necks. Barbara shivered. She felt an evil presence in that temple. Never, she determined, would she set foot inside one.

Soon Barbara settled into her new job in New Delhi as an assistant to the houseparents of teenage children of diplomats. Even though she was teaching at the American high school, she wore the Indian dress of long, billowy pants topped by a slim chemise and a flowing scarf around her neck. In the midst of so much idolatry and paganism, so many, many people who were lost, Barbara's faith was being tested.

During a visit to see friends at the Christian Medical Mission in Madras, Barbara came across a family living in a small, low hut that had a hole in the roof for smoke to escape. The hut was so full of smoke she didn't dare enter. Inside, a mother who was blind had put amulets around her baby's wrists, so tight they were cutting into the child's flesh. Barbara had to do something. Through an interpreter, she asked if she could take the child to see a doctor. There, they bathed her and cut off the rawhide strings. Later Barbara learned that the little girl had died.

Lord, I can't understand. I'm so overwhelmed. There's so much darkness and poverty! Why, Lord, why?

Six months passed. Unfortunately, the extension on Barbara's visa was denied, so she boarded a train crowded with families and their bundles of food and luggage and headed west across the vast stretches of desert. She was on her way back to Israel.

Barbara gazed out the window at the scenery flying by. Scores, even hundreds, of lost people were blurred in her vision as the train sped west. She leaned on her elbow and prayed, *Jesus, there are so many who don't know You! Thank You for each missionary, each believer who is sharing Your love with these people. But what about the ones who don't hear? Will You take care of them?*

With the poverty and darkness of India behind her, Barbara was glad to be returning to the Promised Land. It was good to see her friends on the kibbutz, but Barbara didn't plan to stay long. It was 1964, and soon her sister Marilyn joined her. They headed to Greece. Their first stop was Athens—they walked all over the Acropolis, in and out of temples, visited Mars Hill, and journeyed to the cities of Corinth and Thessalonica, places where the New Testament church had its beginnings.

From there, Barbara and Marilyn traveled on to Norway where they stayed a few days with a friend they had met at the kibbutz, then found jobs with the families of American officers. They attended the American Lutheran church while they were there and were able to share their Christian experience with an international group of young adults. The following year was a whirlwind of cross-country skiing, hiking the fjords, visiting Germany and the Berlin Wall, and traveling to the eastern sector. While in the Communist country, Barbara witnessed firsthand the way atheism ravaged souls, dulling and damaging spiritual senses.

And still the questions haunted her. *God, there is so much suffering in the world, so much pain and hopelessness! Where are You for these people?*

Little wonder that Barbara landed in Switzerland at L'Abri, Dr. Francis Schaeffer's study center in the Alps above Luzanne. It was her deep desire to increase her Christian worldview, to be exposed to apologetics, and to find answers to the many questions raised in her world travels. At lunch and dinner there were discussions with Dr. Schaeffer, and there were special times with Edith Schaeffer, too.

But questions continued to haunt Barbara: Why would God allow so much suffering in the world? Why did the good people, the innocent, suffer so much more than the evil and corrupt? Where were God's justice and mercy? How could His goodness be reconciled with the fact that thousands were perishing . . . and so many of them children? Such hard-hitting questions as these had begun to tarnish the glow of the world's romance and adventure.

And so, Barbara would lean forward at discussion time and pose question after question, always hoping for that elusive answer that would allow her to understand it all and put her mind at rest.

She was not at all prepared for the manner in which God would one day address her questions.

In 1965, Barbara reluctantly returned to America. She had been gone for three years, and it was not easy to fit back into the American culture—especially in southern California. But a close friend introduced Barbara to her brother, and immediately Barbara was swept away by the attentions and affections of this man. Within the next few months, world adventurer Barbara Carey became family adventurer Barbie Kolar.

During the next six years, Barbie and her husband had three children—Kimberly, Lance, and Troy—plus an adopted little girl from Cambodia—Kouy Tha. Family life was a merry-go-round of church and community activities, athletic programs, school events, tennis, and trips throughout the United States and Europe. Life was neat, tidy, orderly, and predictable. The dangers she saw during her long-ago travels seemed, well, long ago. At night Barbie would lie peacefully in bed next to her husband in their quiet, darkened house, with all the children safely tucked in their beds. Life was good.

At least on the surface. Barbie had no idea how difficult her marriage would become. She found it hard to submit to a controlling husband, and there were many spats and disagreements. Then in the early eighties, she discovered her husband was having an affair. Suddenly all the problems and pain and disappointments she had seen out in the world were all too close to home. Her questions about suffering were no longer theoretical. Now they were very, very personal.

Through the crushing disappointment, Barbie clung to the Lord. On her refrigerator she placed a picture of a girl walking up a narrow, dark, winding staircase, holding a candle to light her way. The caption read, "Come higher!" This was her heart's desire.

Together, Barbie and her husband began to work on their marriage.

Then in July of 1984, Barbie took another unexpected step on that dark, winding staircase. Thirteen-year-old Lance brought so much joy to his mother. He was working on becoming an Eagle Scout, loving Christ, filling his sketchbook with drawings, and hoping to study architecture. One day he rode his bike to the pool at the high school to practice swimming and water polo with the team for which he and his brother swam. While fooling around on the pool deck after practice, Lance threw one of his brother's socks up on the roof of the dressing room. Joking and teasing, he scrambled up the chain-link fence to retrieve the sock. As Lance reached for the sock, he suddenly fell through a rotten piece of plywood that was covering a broken skylight. When Barbie drove up to the school, she was greeted by sirens and blinking lights. Lance had fallen on his head. He was rushed to the hospital and put on a respirator. For eight days he remained in a coma.

Barbie stood by her son's bed, unable to sleep or eat for days. Life was a nightmare. She prayed and pleaded; she begged God to spare her son. The doctors performed brain surgery, but after the eighth day, the CAT scan showed a flat line. Lance was brain-dead.

After the funeral, Barbie slowly sank into depression. Between the summer of 1984 and early 1986, life was a dark and turbulent narrow staircase that spiraled ever downward. She was alone in her weeping and in her many visits to her son's grave.

In the spring of 1986, unable to accept his wife's need to work through Lance's death, Barbara's husband chose to leave.

In her mind, Barbie went back to those same questions: Why would God allow so much suffering? Where were God's justice and mercy? Her husband and her son were gone forever.

Barbie's oldest child, Kimberly, graduated from the same high school Lance would have attended, and in 1985 she entered Biola University. Then she, too, began a downward spiral. "My rose-colored glasses were shattered," she wrote as she explained her disillusionment over her brother's death and her parents' separation. She medicated her pain with legal and illegal drugs and alcohol. She became high-risk, moving in and out of hospitals and emergency rooms.

"Suffering keeps crushing our hopes that earth can ever really satisfy, that it can keep its promises."

On May 7, 1988—Barbie's birthday—Kimberly came to see her mother. Kim was quiet that night. Finally she said, "Mom, I'm going into the hospital again tomorrow . . . and I'm scared."

"I'll be there for you," Barbie promised. "I love you, Kim."

The next day Kimberly came by with a Mother's Day card for Barbie, but she left without her mom seeing her. And she never went to the hospital.

Two days later, on May 9, a police car drove up. Kim had crashed her car and was dead at the age of twenty-one. Barbie, who had been in the kitchen making lunches for her children, stared out the kitchen window in numb grief. Her son, Troy, walked out of the house. Her daughter Kouy looked up and said, "Am I next?"

The pain seemed impossible to endure. It was piercing at times. Dull and numb at others. Everything was darkness. Questions piled upon questions. More pain, more perplexity. Nagging doubts. A desperate need to make sense of senseless tragedy. That year was a dark night of the soul.

Some months later, Kouy went to live with her father and his new wife. Troy and Barbie—and a niece who came to live with them—now faced life together in a large, empty home that had once held an active, growing family of six.

Over the next few years, Barbie did not rush into a search for answers. The questions were too overwhelming. How, or to what extent, had God "caused" or "allowed" her divorce and the death of two children? Not only that, but how about the suffering of all the people she had seen in India? And in East Germany?

Why does God allow such suffering?

Yet deep in her mind, Barbie knew this was not really the point. No, the point was that God Himself was the answer to all questions. Barbie needed Him more than ever. And she knew it.

She mused on those early, idealistic days of first coming to Christ. What a longing she'd had to see His world! How she'd wanted to understand the Lord, to appreciate His passion for the lost. A gentle smile crossed her face when she thought again of her favorite verse: "I will never leave thee, nor forsake thee."

He seemed to be whispering, "Come higher, Barbie. Come higher."

"I am Your servant, God. I will go and do whatever You want," Barbie said out loud and through her tears.

In 1996 Barbie, along with her sisters and their families, moved to Colorado.

Now, tucked near the base of the Rockies, Barbie Kolar can look out her window and see Pikes Peak. Many mornings she gazes at the mountain's strong presence and recites with confidence, "'Where does my help come from? My help comes from the LORD, the Maker of heaven and earth'" (Ps. 121:1–2).

Barbie is involved with missions: Campus Crusade, Joni and Friends, Josh McDowell's outreach. She travels and prays, gives and supports. She volunteers at Outreach of Hope, a cancer encouragement ministry. She visits those who are dying, listens to their questions, and gives them permission to express their doubts. She empathizes, identifies, sympathizes, and travails on their behalf. She has won the right to be heard by those who are hurting.

And what about all those questions—especially her own?

Barbie would say, "The Christian life is not the neat and tidy, orderly and predictable life we would like it to be. Nor is it always a life of romance and adventure. The problem of suffering is not about something that can be easily answered. It is about Someone; and so it stands to reason that the answer must be Someone, and not some-thing. *He* is the answer.

"Suffering keeps crushing our hopes that earth can ever really satisfy, that it can ever keep its promises. I've learned not to get too comfortable in a world destined for destruction," Barbie says.

> *"I've learned not to get too comfortable in a world destined for destruction."*

"I remember the time I felt so at home in the land of the Bible. But one day I'll be in the real Promised Land, home at last with my Lord . . . and with all my children. My name—Barbara—means 'stranger,' and I am a stranger here, a pilgrim on my way to the place my Savior is preparing for me. As Psalm 84 says, 'Blessed are those whose strength is in you, who have set their hearts on pilgrimage. As they pass through the [valley of tears], they make it a place of springs . . . They go from strength to strength, till each appears before God in Zion.'

"I wanted to know Jesus before, back when I was young. He answered my heart's desire. But I didn't have to travel all over the world to find Him. He's here, even in my pain. I know Him in the fellowship of sharing in His sufferings. I would never have chosen the path my life has taken; then again, no one necessarily likes taking up his cross daily. But loss forces me to do that every day, and in so doing, I feel His touch on my wounds. And *that* is enough."

At first Barbie was uneasy when I asked if I could write about her in this book. She didn't think her faith was extraordinary enough—after all, she still wrestles with doubts and discouragement. But I think that's exactly what makes her testimony so striking. She reminds me of a song I once sang . . .

Father, set my soul sailing like a cloud upon the wind
Free and strong to carry on until the journey's end.
Each mile I put between the past, and the future in Your hand,
I learn more of your Providence and I find out who I am.

I want to thank you for the gift of Your Son
And for the mystery of prayer,
And for the faith to doubt, and yet believe
That You're really there.[1]

Oh, would that more of us had the faith to doubt and yet believe. Now *that* would be extraordinary.

Consider it pure joy, my brothers, whenever you face trials of many kinds, because you know that the testing of your faith develops perseverance. Perseverance must finish its work so that you may be mature and complete, not lacking anything.

JAMES 1:2–4

7

YET WILL I TRUST
HIM . . . AND PERSEVERE

*E*very day letters pour in to our office. There's no way I can possibly review them all, but I do take time to read a sampling. Those letters are important to me because they keep the questions, concerns, and encouragements from people who read my books fresh in my heart. I am always touched by what folks are experiencing and learning, their struggles, and their growing faith, trust, and confidence in Christ. I receive thousands of letters from people in nursing homes, and there is always a chord that resonates in my heart when I read of their backgrounds, their histories, the countries they've come from, the homes and families they no longer see. And I wonder . . .

Deanna Wolff and Herb Kliewer

What are they learning now?

What new things are they experiencing?

Who are their friends?

How is God still working, still refining, still maturing them?

Is their purpose confined to sitting in their rooms in front of television sets, or is there something more, someone more?

One of the letters I was privileged to read was from a man named Herb Kliewer. Though I have yet to meet him personally, I feel as though I truly know this man who understands firsthand what it means to persevere.

Throughout his life Herb has shifted from pillar to post, uprooted from one town to the next—either forced or fleeing, always moving or being moved, always wondering why. And always, it seems, looking for home. Certainly he was always looking for some purpose for his life.

Not far away lived a young wife and mother, a self-described "country woman," by the name of Deanna Wolff. She, too, was on a journey. Suffering from a serious case of the suburban doldrums, Deanna was badly in need of renewed purpose in her own life. So she made her way to Lynden Manor Assisted Living Residence, a modest building nestled in the foothills of the snowy Cascade Mountains. She liked what she saw. In front, pink roses swayed in full bloom, and the back patio was shaded by towering oaks.

Deanna walked up to the front desk and said, "I want to volunteer. Do you have anything for me to do?"

Like most nursing homes, Lynden's staff cannot keep up with

the workload. You can be sure they accepted Deanna's offer and lost no time in putting her to work.

After several weeks of pitching in here and there, Deanna was approached in the hallway by the activities director. "Would you be willing to do a Bible study for our residents a time or two?" she asked. "Maybe even once a month?"

"I'd love to," Deanna said, "but not once a month. How about once a week?"

When Deanna arrived at her assigned room the first morning, she was greeted by a dozen men and women all decked out in their best clothes, sitting around a table. They had their Bibles and they were eager to begin.

As Deanna gazed around the circle, she couldn't help noticing a large man in a wheelchair. His huge shoulders hunched slightly as though he didn't want to be too obvious. In his beefy hands he clasped a well-worn Bible. When she asked him his name, he answered, "Herb Kliewer," in a rich baritone thick with a German accent.

After a couple of weeks, Herb stayed behind after Bible study and hesitantly asked Deanna, "I was wondering . . . if you had time, could you . . . maybe sometime would you . . . help me with something?"

"Of course," Deanna said. "What do you need?"

Herb took Deanna to his room and showed her a cafeteria table piled high with many books, an assortment of photos, and a stack of papers stapled into sections. Along the back of the table were literally hundreds of colored three-ring folders, all sorted and arranged in piles.

"It's my life," Herb told her. "I want to share it with others . . . what Jesus did for me. I've always wanted to tell people about Jesus, but I didn't know how. So I wrote it down. Will you fix it for me?"

Taking up the top page Deanna began to read: *I was born in a German village in Poland in 1939. My family was farmers who had lived there for many, many years . . .*

Little Herb was only five when Nazi soldiers marched into their village snatching up men to fight the advancing Russians. His father was pressed into service. It didn't matter that he was German; he lived in Poland so he might as well be Polish. Immediately the German neighbors they had known all their lives rushed in and seized the family farm. His mother, aunts, and grandfather were forced to work as slaves on their own farm.

"If you want the rights of Germans, go to Germany!" they told the family. "Anyway, the Russians are coming, and when they get here they'll kill everyone."

In the dark of the night, a Polish farmer loaded all the Kliewers' belongings onto his wagon and took the family to where they could catch a train to Germany. Grandpa (Opa) Kliewer helped the women and children off the wagon, but before he could get their belongings off, the farmer whipped the horses around and drove them away. Everything they owned was gone! Every single thing except the clothes on their backs.

"Never mind," Mother told the frightened children. "We'll be in Germany in two days. Then we'll be all right."

But the station was already crowded with people. The train was so overloaded that not another person could be wedged in.

People were piled on the top and people were hanging off the sides. Everywhere frightened German citizens were pushing and yelling and fighting in their desperation to get on board. Frantic children, separated from their parents, screamed for help. Herb's Opa tried to fight his way onto the train, but it was impossible. There was nothing to do but wait and pray that another one would eventually come.

Finally another train did arrive, and the family was able to get on board. "We'll soon be in Germany," Herb's mother assured her weary children. "It's almost over."

But after only a few miles the train stopped and everyone was ordered off. With so many desperate people and almost no shelter, finding a place to wait for another train seemed hopeless. But eventually Opa managed to find a wooden shack where the family could live until they could resume their journey. It had a leaky roof and no indoor plumbing, but for now it would have to be home.

Life in the makeshift camp was dreadful.

"Every day we saw men hauling wagonloads of dead bodies from somewhere. They threw them around like sacks of potatoes, and then buried them in mass graves."

Some days even basic survival seemed next to hopeless. Herb and his brother Henry went from house to house begging for food, but no one else had anything either. Several times someone discovered a potato field that had just been harvested, and they all scoured every row and dug deep into the dirt in hopes of finding a few leftover potatoes. When they were successful, Opa made a watery soup in an old helmet he had found.

"Oh, my goodness, that soup tasted good!" Herb told Deanna. "I can remember to this day how delicious it was!"

Weeks went by before another train came that they could get on. But it went only a short way before it stopped, and once again everyone was ordered off.

After several more short train rides, each with a long wait in between, the family finally made it across the border into Germany. What should have been a two-day trip took three full months.

But life in Germany was little better. The Kliewers lived in a large dance hall along with fifty other families. Herb's mother tried to make their family a separate room by hanging black army blankets on wires around their small space, but they could still hear every footstep, every word spoken, every cough, every baby's cry.

"For years and years we didn't know whether Father was dead or alive," Herb said. "Many people from the dance hall headed for Canada, the United States, or Uruguay. Even Opa and my aunts finally left. But Mother told us, 'Daddy is coming back someday. We will stay right here and wait for him.' So we waited. And we prayed."

Mother was right. Years later, Herb's father did come back— thin, frail, and wracked with fits of coughing. After years in a Russian prison camp, his captors finally decided he was so near death they might as well let him go.

"When Father came home, everyone sang and cheered to welcome him," Herb said. "Everyone except my youngest brother, Willie. He hadn't seen Father for so long he didn't know who he was. The sight of that strange, skinny man with his bones sticking out scared him."

Herb's father was sent to a hospital where he was treated for tuberculosis. All during his long stay there, Mrs. Kliewer prayed. She prayed that her husband would be healed. She prayed for protection for her children. And she prayed that the family would one day have a home.

God heard her prayers, and Herb's dad was finally released. He immediately went to work and saved every penny so the family could move out of the dance hall where they had been for ten years. The first place they moved to was just a shack, but at least it was their own—and it had running water.

One day, without warning, fifteen-year-old Herb suddenly fell to the floor and lay there. No one knew what to do.

"He's dead!" his sister wailed.

Slowly he came around. But from that day on, whether he took medicine or not, he had one seizure after another. It was the beginning of a lifelong battle with epilepsy.

"The first few years were terrible. Everyone in my family had to watch me to see that I didn't hurt myself. And at night, I had to sleep in my parents' room with them."

One day a missionary came to visit, and with his help and teaching, Herb accepted Christ. "I had been looking and looking for something, but I didn't know what," Herb told Deanna. "I will never, never forget that day!"

Two years later, the family immigrated to the United States. When they landed in New York, seventeen-year-old Herb was confounded by the babbling all around him. No one's talk made any sense. Herb didn't speak a word of English.

From New York the Kliewers went to Oklahoma where their sponsoring family lived. On Sunday they went to church to worship God and thank Him for protecting them and bringing them to this new land. Suddenly, right there in church, a man marched up to them and loudly berated the family in German. Pointing to Herb's father, he yelled, "The war was your fault!"

Furious, Herb and his brother jumped up, determined to protect their father. They wanted to take the man outside and fight him. "No!" their father said, and he went right back to worshiping. The family went back the next Sunday, and every Sunday after that. The United States was their home now, and God would take care of them.

In Oklahoma, the family learned the tortuous art of cotton picking. They spent long days plucking the downy cotton from its razor-sharp boll and dropping it into the huge sacks they dragged behind them. The hot summer sun beat down on them, and the cotton bolls ripped their fingers. Every inch of their bodies ached, yet they dared not slow down. A full cotton sack weighed eighty pounds, and a worker was paid just two cents a pound.

By winter, they had saved enough to move to a small town in Washington. They built a chicken house and filled it with plump hens and a rooster. Then they made a huge garden with plenty of room for potatoes. They planted enough food to last them the entire year—and that was a lot! Herb and his two sisters and three brothers had known so much hunger that they just could not get enough to eat. They ate and ate and ate some more. When they went to school, they ate their own lunches then they ate the other children's leftover sandwiches and apples. After that they ate the bread crusts and the apple cores and any other scraps.

Herb was eighteen years old, but because he knew so little English, he was put into fourth grade with children half his size. His favorite subject? "Lunch! I didn't learn much, but I sure did eat."

Three years later the family moved again, this time to Seattle. But Herb—now twenty—didn't go along. A man at church named Leonard had hired him to work at his dairy. Leonard knew all about Herb's struggles with epilepsy.

"That won't be a problem here," he told Herb.

Herb still couldn't speak English.

"Doesn't matter to me," Leonard said. "I speak German."

In exchange for working on the farm and milking the cows, Leonard gave Herb a comfortable room in the attic, three dollars a day, and—best of all—all the food he could eat. "I never ate so good!" Herb told Deanna. "I could eat three or four hamburgers at a time—sometimes even five!"

Kids who came to work on the farm in haying season teased Herb about being Polish, about not speaking good English, about not understanding American ways, and even about his epilepsy. "I thought we were friends," Herb said sadly, "but all the time they were making fun of me."

Still, Herb persevered. He was happy on the farm, and Leonard truly was a good friend to him. Finally, it seemed, Herb had a home and life was good.

At long last, Herb took the bus up to Seattle to visit his family for the weekend. Everyone was so excited to see him, and he was absolutely ecstatic to see them. His mother looked great. She couldn't stop hugging and kissing him. His brothers and sisters clapped him on the back between hugs and asked questions faster than he could answer. It was all so wonderful.

But something wasn't right. Where was his father . . . his hero . . . the most important person in his life? He was the one Herb was especially eager to see. How Herb longed to hug him and tell him how much he loved him! But where was he?

It was hard to get away from the hugging and chattering and questions and the dancing young ones, but Herb finally managed to make his way into the house. There, alone in the corner, sat his father.

"Father?" Herb asked. "What's wrong?"

Without looking up, his father began to talk. But his words made no sense. "I got the terrible feeling that my father was losing his mind."

The next day everyone went to work or to school except Herb and his father. Herb got the family Bible from the nightstand in his parents' bedroom and read from it to his father. Then they prayed together. After that they turned on the radio and listened as God's Word was preached. Things seemed much better, almost like old times.

After a couple of hours, Herb's father stood up. "You stay here and finish listening to the radio program," he told Herb. "I'm going outside to get some fresh air."

When the program ended and his father hadn't come back, Herb listened to another program. But when it also ended and his father still wasn't back, Herb decided to go out and look for him.

"Did you see my dad?" Herb called to a neighbor who was mowing his lawn next door.

"He went into the garage about twenty minutes ago," the neighbor called back. "I didn't see him come back out, so I guess he's still in there."

When Herb went into the garage, he found his father lying on the floor—dead. He had asphyxiated himself.

Numb with grief, Herb went back to the farm. He tried to work hard, but his health was worsening. He wanted to live for Jesus, but his brain was reeling with questions and doubts. Why did God let such an awful thing happen? Why had He brought Father home from the war and carried him through such a terrible case of tuberculosis just to have him die like this? If Father had to die now, why couldn't it have been from a heart attack, or in a car accident on his way home from work? Why this way?

The more Herb tried to keep his mind on his work, the more he was plagued by the horror of it all. His father had always been the leader of the family, the one who faithfully gathered everyone together to pray on their knees. He was the one who always talked about the Lord, whose faith never seemed shaken. How could this have happened? And how could Herb go on without him?

Questions and more questions . . . but no answers. His father had been the one with the answers, and now he was gone.

For twenty-five years Herb lived and worked on the farm. Sometimes he wondered what it would be like to have a wife and children of his own, but he knew that was out of the question. He worked such long hours—up to eighteen hours a day in the harvest season. And then there was his illness. How could he ever hope to meet anyone?

The seizures were a constant in his life. Whenever he felt one coming on, he would quickly stop what he was doing and lie down. More times than he could count he had awakened lying in the milk house gutter. He simply got up and finished milking the cows.

In the mid-1980s, the tractor Herb was driving swerved off into a ditch and rolled over on top of him. "The doctor told me I was lucky I survived," Herb said, "but I knew it was God."

"The last few years on the farm weren't so good for me."

That's an understatement. During haying season the following year, Herb fell out of the hayloft and broke his back. He recovered fairly well. But then he lost his balance while unloading bales of hay, fell backward onto the wagon hitch, and broke his neck. That left him totally paralyzed.

After five long months in the hospital, forty-nine-year-old Herb was moved to a nursing home. Sharing a room with three other men with only a curtain separating them brought back haunting memories of living in the dance hall in Germany. He also thought about his godly father, but those good memories were quickly replaced with bitter ones of that horrible day in the garage.

Then came the old nagging questions about God.

"Those days were very dark for me," Herb told Deanna. "I had to struggle to keep from losing my mind."

Day after day he lay in bed staring blankly into the air. How much he had been through! Yet, in it all, he had trusted God and persevered. So why had it come down to this?

One depressing thought crowded out all others: *There is nothing left of me but broken pieces, just worthless broken pieces. What good am I now?*

Like Job of old, Herb begged to understand.

"Why can't I be healthy and strong to serve You, Lord?" he cried. "So many times I've clung to the very last string, just hoping You would call me home. But You didn't. Why do You leave me here like this? I'm no good to anyone, not even You. Why, Lord? Why?"

Even with a broken back, Herb smiles

God didn't explain His ways to Herb. Just as He didn't explain to Job. Just as He didn't explain to me. Just as He doesn't explain to you.

But although God didn't explain, He did answer.

"It was almost like Jesus was right there by my bed. He told me, *Broken pieces are all I need. I will put those pieces back together, and I will make something wonderful out of your life.*"

Something wonderful out of nothing but broken pieces! It changed Herb's life. Yes, he was still in his bed. Yes, his body was still broken. Yes, he still suffered from epilepsy. Yes, his English was still poor. But he knew—*knew beyond the shadow of a doubt*—that God was right there with him and was in charge. Hopelessness faded in the bright light of assurance. God *would* make something wonderful out of his life.

Jesus told me,

Broken pieces

are all I need.

I will put

those pieces

back together.

As if to seal His promise, God allowed the feeling to slowly come back to Herb's hands, and then to his arms. No longer is his entire body paralyzed.

"Only my legs and stomach don't work now. The rest of my body has feelings. I can move from my bed to my wheelchair without any help. I wheel around and go wherever I want."

As soon as he learned to hold a pen again, Herb set about copying Bible verses that were especially meaningful to him. But his room gave him too little privacy. And there were so many distractions that it was hard for him to focus. "I asked the nurses for help, and they gave me a room in the basement that wasn't being used in the afternoons. Down there I could concentrate on my lessons."

I love the fact that the Bible was and is so important to Herb. Deanna was impressed by that, too; it is also very important to her.

Out of all his treasured Bible verses, Herb's favorite is John 3:16: "For God so loved the world, that he gave his only begotten Son, that whosoever believeth in him should not perish, but have everlasting life" (KJV).

Deanna has a favorite verse, too . . . Romans 8:28: "And we know that all things work together for good to those who love God, to those who are the called according to His purpose" (NKJV).

I wholeheartedly echo Herb's and Deanna's appreciation of both verses. They're favorites of mine as well. And I would go on to add more of Romans 8, especially verses 31–32, 35, and 37–38:

What, then, shall we say in response to this? If God is for us, who can be against us? He who did not spare his own Son, but gave him up for us all—how will he not also, along with him, graciously give us all things? . . . Who shall separate us from the love of Christ? Shall trouble or hardship or persecution or famine or nakedness or danger or sword? . . . No, in all these things we are more than conquerors through him who loved us.

For I am convinced that neither death nor life, neither angels
nor demons, neither the present nor the future, nor any powers,
neither height nor depth, nor anything else in all creation, will
be able to separate us from the love of God that is in Christ Jesus
our Lord.

That's it!

God loved us so much that He gave His Son to die for us. For
Herb, a sickly little boy in Poland. For Deanna, a restless country
homemaker in a small Washington town. For you and me, just
exactly where we are and who we happen to be.

He loves us so much that He works everything out for our
good and His glory. Even war-torn homelands and broken bodies, and ordinary people struggling along in ordinary lives, and
"chance" meetings that bring us together with unlikely people.

Once we are His, nothing—*not a single thing in all of heaven
or earth*—can separate us from Him. He puts our broken pieces
together and makes us more than conquerors.

That's why Herb trusts in the Lord. That's why he longs to tell
what Christ did for him. That's why he is able to persevere.

"It's wonderful to be a Christian," Herb told me on the telephone. "Jesus is so good and faithful to me. Every day He blesses me.
I have a large room now here at Lynden Manor. I have a great view
of the mountains and all the freedom I need. And I have Deanna to
help me. My goodness, my cup is running over all the time."

That is also why Deanna trusts God. "Herb has the balcony
view," she says, "and I have a front-row seat. Herb says I've been

a gift to him, but I can tell you, he has been every bit as much a gift to me. I thank God every day that Herb is in my life."

There are millions of people living in nursing homes across the country. And you know what? Every single one of them has a rich history. Every one has a family remembered in sepia photos, framed and sitting on crocheted doilies on cluttered nightstands. They are from all over the world and from distant decades. They carry memories of war, of immigration ships sailing to America, of hunger and need like I have never known, of working in factories and coal mines and on wartime assembly lines, of long-ago families peopled with laughing children and loved ones long gone. They hold the memories of times and places that are no more. They also carry the memories of faith and faithfulness through times of persecution and terrible suffering.

One's purpose in life doesn't depend on understanding God's plan, but how we respond to a tough circumstance right now, this day, this instant.

And what about Deanna? She is just one of a multitude of privates in the army of the Lord who faithfully labor on forgotten fields. Many people dismiss their ministries as too unglamorous and too unimportant to matter. But that doesn't bother people like Deanna. They neither expect nor desire praise and glory. To the people at Lynden Manor, Deanna is a best friend and the closest thing to family many of them have.

She brings sunshine to their Monday mornings, and it continues to shine throughout their week.

Herb and Deanna have taught me a wonderful lesson in perseverance. Of going on when I don't think I can anymore . . . when I think it's useless. Of faithfully doing that which God gives me to do . . . even if it seems unimportant. Even if nobody notices . . . or praises me . . . or thanks me. They've shown me that one's purpose in life doesn't depend on understanding God's plan or why He allowed awful—or even good—things to happen. God's purpose is more often focused on the moment, on how we respond to a tough circumstance right now, this day, this instant. His grand purpose in our lives is usually played out through the everyday and the oh-so-ordinary relationships in which we find ourselves. A simple and unpretentious relationship, such as that which Herb and Deanna enjoy.

Herb and Deanna have taught me to steadfastly keep on keeping on. In other words, to persevere.

Let us not become weary in doing good, for at the proper time we will reap a harvest if we do not give up.

GALATIANS 6:9

8

YET WILL I TRUST
HIM . . . AND BE FAITHFUL

*B*lond hair and blue eyes, tall and sweet-spirited, as fresh and sunny as the cornfield next to his home on Old Court Road. That's my friend Craig Garriott. He and his brother used to come to my house for Bible studies when I was struggling to find answers. Oh, how patient, kind, and long-suffering he was, especially when handling the tough questions I threw his way. It was hard to wave good-bye when he left for Virginia Polytechnic Institute.

After he graduated, Craig went on to seminary. Next I heard he was—what?!—pastoring a missions church in the inner city? Craig and his new wife? Straight-from-the-country Craig? At first it didn't sound at all like a fit—especially some years later when I read a couple of newspaper articles his wife, Maria, had written for the *Baltimore Sun*. For instance, this one was entitled "Hoop Dreams and Hard Realities."

My husband took the basketball hoop down last night. We had seen it coming for a long time. The boys from our Pen Lucy neighborhood kept hanging on the rim, bending the metal until the backboard tilted over precariously and threatened to fall on their heads. We asked them repeatedly not to hang on the rim, told them rim-hangers would be kicked off the court, that the backboard would eventually break and then no one

Craig and Maria Garriott

would be able to play anymore. But they wouldn't listen, couldn't or wouldn't control themselves. Their heroes, Charles and Shaq and Magic, all hang on the rim.

Perhaps it was doomed from the start. My husband pastors a church in our urban neighborhood, and we know how scarce recreational space is in the inner city. Once a week, he takes a vanload of youths to a gym several miles outside our neighborhood. It's a great time to build relationships, to meet on common ground, to invest in the lives of young men in the hope that some of them will be encouraged in the right direction.

"We really need a gym," my husband says wistfully almost every week. He so wishes our church had the resources to build such a treasure. But church finances are stretched tight and no gym money is in sight.

So we built a half court in our backyard. Two summers ago, with our home still half renovated, we took money that should have gone toward putting in a back door or paying our children's school tuition and bought a dumptruck-load of concrete. My husband laid out the court himself, measuring and digging and laying down rebar. They trundled the concrete in wheelbarrows into the backyard, and a neighbor smoothed it carefully. My husband put up an adjustable backboard so that our young son and other small boys could know the thrill of making baskets.

There were problems from the start. We would look outside and see ten or fifteen older guys—most of whom we had never met—playing while the younger boys from our block sat idle on the picnic table. The big guys would hang on the rim, leave candy wrappers and soda cans lying around, and trample the few lonely flowers I had planted. Careless, but not malicious.

But someone broke the sump pump line that juts out of our basement. They jumped up and down on the PVC pipe until it shattered. Twice. So my husband had to spend two more Saturday mornings fixing that. The boys were loud and boisterous, and we wondered how much our neighbors could take. We would shut the gate to the backyard and they would climb over it. We bought a lock and chained the gate shut but they would run through the neighbors' yard and climb over the fence. We would return home from work or from an outing to the endless slapping of leather on concrete, of leather banging against the rim.

We posted hours: *Basketball from 4:00 to 6:00* read the hand-lettered signs on the fence. The signs were torn down and everyone professed ignorance. In desperation, my husband built a new gate, wooden and ten feet high, with no latch on the outside. The boys just climbed over the fence and unlocked it. When confronted, the story was the same, "We didn't open it; there was guys already here when we got here."

We fluctuated between frustration, anger, resentment, resignation, and hope. We watched Joe, an older youth who came often to play, leave off playing ball and fall in with the drug dealers who occupy the corner house. He sat on his porch, front door open and stereo blasting, getting high.

"Joe, come play some ball," I would invite. It was better to put up with the inconvenience and the noise, and try to build relationships, hoping some of these guys would be influenced for good.

We remembered some of the young men who grew up in our church youth group, playing ball with youth group leaders who had become Christians. They graduated from high school, got jobs, and became husbands and fathers, even though they hadn't known their own fathers. It would be worth it all to see just one boy go the right way.

But our basketballs wore out or disappeared. The rim started hanging, and yesterday we looked outside to see it propped up with a long board the kids found behind the house. "Chris was hanging on the rim and broke it," the younger boys said. We found Chris, and he maintained his ignorance; the little boys had done it. Well, it's done now, I told him. Now no one can play. His face was blank, feigning indifference.

Last night, my husband dragged out the stepladder and took the ailing backboard off. The pole remains, jutting upward out of a sea of concrete like an impotent mast. The backyard is quiet.

An hour later, we heard the familiar sound of gunshots from the corner. My children called me from their beds. My eight-year-old son, swaddled in blankets on the floor near his sister's bed, grumped, "We hear gunshots almost every night. And the police never come." But the police did come, and we could see the red lights flashing rhythmically against our neighbor's house.

I couldn't help thinking about our basketball court. Maybe if there were more recreational areas where boys could work off steam. Maybe if there were more fathers, like our neighbor Cornell Pierce who came occasionally with his boys to play. His sons were respectful, delightful, the obvious fruit of a strong father's investment. Maybe if our church had more money to hire youth workers to spend time with vulnerable kids. Maybe if I didn't have to work two part-time jobs to pay tuition so that my children could escape the sinking ship of urban public schools. Maybe if the boys hadn't destroyed the court. Maybe . . .

Maria Garriott

Faith Christian Fellowship

Baltimore City[1]

I put down the article and closed my eyes. *How in the world do Craig and Maria find the energy to go on?* I wondered. *How can they remain so faithful?* Then I pondered, *Why burn yourself out in the city? Why this waste?*

You might think the same.

Actually, so did Craig and Maria.

Fresh out of seminary, young and energetic, Craig had been convinced that Jesus was the answer for the world, and for the city, with its racial strife, social injustices, and hungry souls. He had responded to a call to become the organizing pastor of a mission church in a low-income section of Baltimore.

A grace-filled, Spirit-driven church could make a difference. Things don't have to be the way they are! Craig thought as he and his young wife, Maria, plastered a huge map of Baltimore on the wall. Lettered over the top was "The Baltimore Vision" and Proverbs 29:18 (KJV) was written underneath: *"Where there is no vision, the people perish."* Craig was a half-baked seminarian with football bravado—as he puts it—and he told God, "Yeah, bring it on! If You want me to give my life for the city, here I am!"

In 1981 Craig, Maria, and their two-week-old baby moved into a three-story apartment house on the 3500 block of Greenmount Avenue in Baltimore. Grass was two feet high in the front yard. The heat didn't work, the roof leaked, and lead paint had to be scraped off the window frames. The house had the reputation of being a slum-lord-owned drug house—a far cry from Craig's home twenty miles away in cornfield country. Yet it was there that they were planted.

When Craig prayed for leaders to work alongside him, God brought two men: Bill Bolling, a Christian who fought his way up out of the slums to graduate from Virginia Tech, and Bob Jenkins, a former skid-row panhandler who had been in and out of jails until he was convicted by Christ and eventually became a prominent lawyer. When God connected these street-smart leaders to Craig and several other leaders, they were on their way.

When people of different races and backgrounds come together in worship, the wattage goes up on God's glory.

Craig dived in to lead this mismatched band of energized believers. They set up camp in the old Boundary United Methodist Church building and called their new church Faith Christian Fellowship. In those early days, Craig saw God move mountains as his small church slowly began to come together: a church comprised of blacks and whites, rich and poor, street folks who wandered in still high on drugs, teenage mothers, and kids who chose Christ rather than gangs. There were also college students from nearby Johns Hopkins University and Morgan State University who wanted a faith that addressed society's dilemmas. Craig and the team operated a daycare center, a legal clinic, a juvenile prison ministry, a counseling outreach, and a food and clothing pantry—all with less than fifty helpers.

But after a while the enthusiasm of the early years began to wane as some of the hardest-working members of his team began to struggle with exhaustion. Programs faltered for lack of resources, and volunteers were burned out. Families and leaders, who faced the crushing challenges of raising and educating kids in the city, left. Others were sick and tired of having their apartments burglarized. There were always addicts on the street asking for handouts. There were slit tires and graffiti. There was the euphoria of seeing new converts come off drugs and then the disappointment of seeing them fall back. What was most heartbreaking was to see blacks and whites still preferring their comfort zones; people of different classes and races remained separated.

By 1987, Craig found himself up against a wall. He and Maria were trying to raise four children under the age of seven in a neighborhood with depleted resources and growing violence. The low point came when the police called Craig to identify the body of Steve Stahl, a white man in his early forties who had been the very first convert at Faith Christian Fellowship and had become one of the first deacons. Yet Steve could not "shake the demons off his back," and he ended up jumping off the Forty-first Street Bridge above the Jones Fall Expressway.

As Craig gazed upon Steve's broken and mangled body, he was flooded with deep disappointment and anger. He cried out to God, *So this is what You brought me to the city for? Believers committing suicide? My leaders pulling up stakes and heading out? Blacks and whites unable to come together in Your body? My own wife and kids taking blow after blow?! How can I remain faithful to this call?*

Both Craig and Maria were strongly tempted to flee their crime-ridden community, especially when Craig knew that his peers in the green suburbs were passing the two-hundred-member mark in their resource-rich church plants. He knew he wasn't supposed to focus on numbers, but Faith Christian Fellowship struggled to keep above sixty members. *Maybe this reconciliation vision is just for heaven, 'cause it sure ain't workin' here,* Craig thought with a tinge of bitterness.

That's when God began to answer. At first it was through simple verses like Galatians 6:9: "Let us not become weary in doing good, for at the proper time we will reap a harvest if we do not give up." And 2 Corinthians 4:8–9: "We are hard pressed on every side, but not crushed; perplexed, but not in despair; persecuted, but not abandoned; struck down, but not destroyed." Craig read John 17 and heard the anguish in Jesus' voice when He asked the Father, "I pray . . . that all of them may be one . . . that the world may believe that you have sent me" (vv. 20–21).

Craig asked himself, "Does the Bible speak to the issues that have caused the exodus of hundreds of thousands of residents from the city? Does it speak to the tens of thousands who have become addicted to drugs? To soaring rates of murder, illiteracy, unemployment, despair, and apathy?" He heard the answer in Micah 6:8: "He has showed you, O man, what is good. And what does the LORD require of you? To act justly and to love mercy and to walk humbly with your God."

The young pastor dropped to his knees and prayed, "Oh Lord, I see that there is no true worship of You unless there is justice. There is no true witness of the gospel unless there is unity. There is no power in our efforts unless there is a dependence on You through prayer. Help me to stay where You want me to be."

Out of his own crisis, Craig returned to seminary to pursue a doctorate in Urban Missions. From his studies, he realized an important fact: The work of reconciliation will always be messy. It will always be five steps forward and three back. He realized there is no Emily Post picture-perfect congregation, and that when people of different races and backgrounds come together in worship, the wattage goes up on God's glory. It was clear to Craig and Maria—they must be faithful to God's calling.

They dug in once again and moved around the corner from their church to be more present in their Pen Lucy community, a tough, low-income, minority neighborhood of hardworking folks who struggled with gang violence and an entrenched drug problem. Forty percent of its residents were below the poverty threshold, 50 percent of the families were maintained by the mother, and 70 percent of the homes were rental properties.

On the corner of their street a pair of boots had been thrown over the telephone wires, a symbol that drugs were available at that intersection. On the other corner, someone had spray-painted the names of youths whose lives had been cut short: R.I.P. Azhar, Pookie, and other names. The high murder rate in Baltimore was not just statistics—each name was some mother's son, somebody's brother, a neighborhood friend.

And yet there were those who thanked God that Craig and Maria remained faithful.

There's Carneal Means, a handsome, gentle-voiced man who describes himself as a former "hopeless, homeless drunk and cocaine addict for twenty-three years. When you went downtown and saw people sleeping outside, that was me. I've gone into neighborhoods the devil himself wouldn't go into."

In one of these neighborhoods, as Carneal sought out another hit of crack, someone put a shotgun to his back and pulled the trigger. As he lay dying, he asked God for forgiveness. "This was a first for me," he recalls. "Normally I would bargain with God." Miraculously, he woke up twenty-two days later in shock trauma, paralyzed from the waist down. Doctors believed he had a 10 percent chance of survival. His family stayed by him, and his sister prayed and helped him get into a drug program.

One July afternoon he wandered into a Faith Christian Fellowship event Craig was conducting in Mullins Park, the neighborhood drug-dealing center. Carneal was deeply moved, and the following Sunday he came to the worship service. He's been there ever since. Carneal was enfolded into one of the small group Bible studies, eventually becoming a small group leader and head usher

There are others, too. There's Arlette Lindsay, one of the church's founding members, who hosted a home for unwed mothers. There's Pat Taylor, who used to be involved in cults, lived at the YMCA for lack of a home, and now provides strategic leadership in community outreach. And there's Stan Long, an African-American brother who helped establish Faith Christian Fellowship twenty years ago when he was an InterVarsity staff worker and who now teams up with Craig as co-pastor. (Craig and Maria could name tens of faithful urban warriors who have staunchly dug in to the trenches with them, quiet heroes who encouraged their faith.)

And there is still more evidence that the Lord has blessed the

*The Garriott family. Left to right:
Melissa, Calvin, Maria, Caroline,
Rebecca, Juliana, and Craig.*

Garriotts' faithfulness, which has been strengthened by many urban warriors. On a recent December night, three hundred parents and children crammed into the sanctuary for an end-of-the-season soccer award ceremony. It was an opportunity to proclaim Christ through a part of the church's Pen Lucy Youth Partnership program. As proud parents watched their children receive awards, volunteer coaches were recognized and the gospel was proclaimed. Many of these children were a part of the church's after-school tutorial program. A few weeks later, another three hundred children and parents filled the sanctuary for Baltimore Christian School's Christmas program. The school, founded in 1993, provides an excellent Christian education for children regardless of their economic means.

Faith Christian Fellowship has indeed become a fruit-bearing church; in the last year, the church sent out several couples who have been shepherded through seminary and discipled in ministry.

Balance all this against an empty basketball court in Craig's backyard.

A court with a bare pole and no backboard.

Balance this against the dropouts and flopouts and the countless hours invested for which there's not a trace of results. Craig and Maria, Bill and Bob, Stan and Carneal, Arlette and Pat, and scores of others are staying because *results aren't the issue.*

Faithfulness is.

"Well done, good and faithful servant," Jesus will one day say. You have been trustworthy in a few matters, now take charge over ten cities." It's ironic that Jesus chose the word *cities.* It *could* make

Craig laugh—or cry! But it's a fact that spurs Faith Christian Fellowship on. Craig and the team are not looking at success in terms of numbers or results; they are focused on faithfulness to the call.

Craig and Maria and their faithfulness at Faith Christian Fellowship make me realize that I, too, must never grow weary in well-doing. I must hold tight to my own hoop dreams despite the hard realities that come my way. And how about you? Friends, keeping the dream means people like Carneal are coming into the fold. We must keep the dream because the Bible *does* speak to the city's issues. Because acting justly and loving mercy bring glory to the Father. Because we may be perplexed, but we are not in despair; we may be knocked down, but we are not knocked out.

Results aren't the issue. Faithfulness is.

Keep the dream, for in due season you will reap as well as hear the commendation of Christ, saying, "Well done!"

Mrs. Garriott's Neighborhood

by Maria Garriott

When Mr. Brown moved out
the landlord bricked up all the windows
on the alley side
to save money on his insurance

and my son said the police were busting someone
at the corner house
after church on Sunday
but I was busy in the kitchen
and just said uh-huh
and Craig took the neighborhood kids to play basketball
and to McDonalds afterwards
but told our kids not to spoil their appetites
because I was cooking dinner
and Binky said
he wished someone was cooking at his house

and a bullet went through my neighbor's house
and shot him as he lay in bed

and I was tired
and I lay down
and I told Jesus not to wake me up
unless He would carry me

and oh, glory,
He carried me.

I will instruct you and teach

you in the way you should go;

I will counsel you

and watch over you.

PSALM 32:8

9

YET WILL I TRUST
HIM . . . AND OBEY

*W*henever an urgent prayer need crops up, there's a friend I run to: Joan Liggins, who works in data entry for our organization. Everyone around Joni and Friends knows that Joan is a prayer warrior par excellence, and if there's a need for intercession, we know Joan will drop to her knees and lift up the problem before the throne of God. Who's the first to show up at 8:00 A.M. for prayer every morning? Joan. Who prays with passion and fervent devotion? Joan again. Whom do I E-mail if I'm on the road and in need of prayer support? You guessed it.

You might imagine Joan Liggins to be the quiet,

meek, reserved type. Not so. Only 4'11", she is a bundle of boundless energy. When sitting at my desk, I can look over my shoulder and catch Joan, with a basket of mail in hand, scurrying across the courtyard as Edith would on *All in the Family.* She is, as one coworker describes, "an Italian dynamo." When I'm praying with Joan and happen to open my eyes, I always see her leaning forward in her chair, with head bowed and knuckles clutched so tightly, they're white.

When I wheel through the office with visitors and drop by data entry, I sometimes say to Joan Liggins, "Would you tell these folks your story?" And what a story she tells.

Joan grew up in an Italian home in New York where cursing

Joan Liggins

and screaming were always punctuated by a slammed door. Her parents battled constantly, and she, along with her three siblings, frequently took the blow of a fist or the slap of a hand across the face. At night when she would pull the covers around her, she'd feel the anger simmering and smoldering. It didn't help that her parents sent her every Sunday to a church down the road where— as she describes it now—the pastor preached only hellfire and damnation. He would say smugly, "Christians don't smoke, drink, neck, or go to movies. Period." Rules and regulations like these only heightened her rebellion. She despised the drudgery of rule-keeping. She grew to hate the idea of obedience. Yet ironically, that same anger fueled a fiery, competitive spirit by which she won Scripture memory contests and vacation Bible school awards. She was going to make her mark and beat those self-righteous church people at their own game. For a time, she did.

However, her anger and the itchiness to have things go her way squelched any potential friendships. Joan was a good student, but she was constantly getting sent to the office for picking fights with classmates. She ended up hanging around her older brother. Together, they invented all sorts of mischief, from ringing door-bells and running away to stealing small items from the local five-and-dime. Lifting tubes of lipstick off the shelf evolved to shoplifting larger items and, soon, she was arrested and slapped with a year's probation. That only stoked the fire.

Her brother became known as a party animal, always inviting his buddies over to the house when his parents were gone. The lights were low in the basement, the beer flowed, and the hi fi blasted Jerry Lee Lewis and James Brown. Joan didn't know how to dance, but she could tell lies and flirt. And flirting with her older brother's friends led to many a late night on the downstairs sofa.

"That's it!" her mother said as she slapped her hand on the table one day. "You kids are going to be the death of me. We're moving out of here . . . going to California." Joan was stunned. She had come to depend on the sexual attention she was receiving from boys. It gave her significance—a strange kind of power—it was a release for all the anger.

"You can't! You can't do this!" she screamed. The protest erupted into another round of flying fists and slamming doors. Whether Joan liked it or not, at the age of sixteen she was moving to California.

New Yorkers seem to have a bone to pick with Californians, and Joan was no exception. She quickly slipped back into the rut of fighting with classmates. She became known as the hotheaded Italian from New York. Maybe that's why she was drawn to John, the quiet, shy boy from school she met on a blind date. It wasn't that she *liked* John so much as she felt she could control him. Plus, he didn't yell and have a temper—she liked that about him. They dated for two years, and shortly after high school graduation, Joan found herself pregnant. Frustrated and bewildered, she recalled those old rules and regulations and did what she thought was right. She married. She married without a hint of love in her heart.

I've got to do this marriage thing correctly, she thought, especially after her baby, Renee, was born. But juggling childcare, a day job in data entry at Douglas Aircraft in Santa Monica, changing diapers, rushing home, throwing together dinners, and all with a husband who remained quiet, shy, and distant, just as when they dated, was, well . . . fuel for hotter fire. The smallest thing would set her off, like little Renee spilling milk. *Slap!* would go Joan's hand across the child's face. Demoralized, Joan would try harder next time, but her good intentions always shattered into fits of anger against her little girl. She was repeating her parents' mistakes.

Joan became sick of the whole charade at home. Keeping rules was a dead end. She found release at work, and she struck up a friendship with a guy in programming. Unlike John, this man was smooth, chatty, and very handsome. Occasional work lunches together led to secret rendezvous in hotels. Joan was back to her old ways. Her marriage to John was a joke.

"I want a divorce," she told her husband.

"I don't understand," John stammered.

"I mean it. Give me a divorce," she said adamantly.

John looked like a lost puppy. *That's what I can't stand about him,* she thought, *he's insipid. Got no backbone.* Her husband dropped his head, and Joan squirmed a bit. She knew her husband depended on her very much. But the pull of her dark passions was stronger. The divorce went through, and Joan flung herself into a two-year relationship with her coworker

> *God is the Father running down the road to embrace the prodigal before he has spoken a word of contrition.*

in which her life became a numbing blur of drinking, sex, parties, and packs of cigarettes. When her frayed nerves and sensual desires weren't dulled by alcohol and sex, she and her boyfriend fought. Constantly.

Joan hit rock bottom in September of 1968. Her life was in shambles. Thoughts of "ending it all" drifted through her mind. It scared her enough to cause her to scramble and search for an answer. Help. Anything! The weeks that followed were a frantic, furtive search taking her two steps forward and then five steps back, at which point she'd fall into bed with her lover.

That's when the phone call came from her cousin. "Uh, listen, Joan . . . I know you've been going through tough times. Wanna go with me to church on Sunday evening?"

Joan held the receiver tightly to her face but could not bring herself to answer. All the memories of hellfire and damnation, of self-righteous preachers spouting rules and regulations, always saying one thing and doing another, came flooding back. Yet, a gentle, quiet urging—the same quiet nudge that prodded her to marry when she was pregnant—whispered to her, *This one time . . . do something right. Go. Go with your cousin. Go to church.*

A cool November breeze swept down from the Northridge mountains that Sunday evening as Joan and her cousin pulled into the parking lot of the First Baptist Church of Van Nuys. She sat for a moment and watched happy people ambling by with their smiling children in tow. *This place isn't for me,* she thought as a shiver ran through her body. Once inside and settled into the red-cushioned pew, Joan glanced around. *I can't believe how many people are here on a Sunday night. This is incredible.*

The organ began playing, and Joan stood with the others, fumbling to find the right page in the hymnal. The feelings of strangeness began to dissipate as she realized, *Hey, I remember this hymn. I used to sing this back at that church in New York.* After a few more songs, she closed her hymnal and settled back to listen to Dr. Harold Fickett, the pastor.

"Now you may have heard that God can't stand sinners. You may have heard He expects you to come groveling on your knees, begging and pleading for mercy as though He were holding a club behind His back and waiting to bop you over the head. You may have heard that He hates reprobates like you, that He can't wait to punish a person for drinking and sex and divorce—"

Joan froze. *That's me.* She eyed her cousin sitting placidly next to her. *Did she tell this preacher about me?!*

Dr. Fickett continued, pointing to the open Bible on his pulpit. "But I am here to tell you that 'this is the love of God: in that while we were yet sinners, Christ died for us.' God is the Father running down the road to embrace the prodigal before He has spoken a word of contrition. God is the Great Shepherd who leaves the ninety-nine in the field to go out searching for that one lost sheep."

Joan felt her cheeks flush. Her breathing became short, her mind alert. She felt an eerie warmth fill her heart. *I've never heard God portrayed this way.*

The sermon seemed to fly by with Joan hanging on every

word. Finally, Dr. Fickett closed his Bible, walked to the side of the altar, and faced the audience with his hands behind his back. "You may have felt like a black sheep up until tonight. You may have thought you were too sinful, too stubborn for God to forgive. You may be afraid you won't be able to really change. I'm telling you not to let those things get in the way. The Lord Jesus Christ, that Great Shepherd of the sheep, has died on the cross for you and, if you believe, if you place your trust in Him tonight, you will escape the wrath that is coming, and you will be transformed into God's dear child. Come," Dr. Fickett said softly. "Come forward and receive Jesus tonight."

Organ music began to play, ushers quietly moved to the front, and Joan felt herself rise to her feet. She had heard similar appeals in that little church back in New York; she even recognized the same organ music. But this was new. This time she felt utterly overwhelmed not only by her sin, but by the compelling love of Christ calling her, "Oh, sinner, come home." Joan swiftly moved out of the pew, stumbling past her cousin, and virtually scurried—like Edith in *All in the Family*—down the carpeted aisle to kneel at the front. It was, for her, a dramatic conversion. She prayed, stood up with tears dripping from her cheeks, breathed deeply, and smiled. Joan *knew* her life had changed.

They say the first gifts that God gives to a brand-new believer are saving faith and a spirit of repentance. The part about faith was evident—that night Joan felt the chains of sin literally break and fall away, leaving her feeling fresh and free. Repentance was also evident—immediately many Bible verses from childhood came flooding back, some of which were about marriage and divorce. Before that Sunday night was over, she knew what she must do. It was an almost unbelievable decision . . .

She must remarry her ex-husband. A man she did not love. *And I must marry John because of my love for God. I must . . . no, I want to obey.*

The clear evidence of Joan's dramatic conversion was the fact that the very next month—in December of 1968—Joan and John were remarried. She peered at her husband as they stood together at the altar. *He seems so glad, as though nothing ever happened. He's still the same person . . . and I still don't like him,* she thought. *But I'm not the same person. I am a Christian now, and I want to obey God, trusting that He will bless our marriage. Oh, God,* she prayed, *bless our marriage.*

"God *will* bless your decision to remarry your husband," said Allegra, Joan's new Bible study teacher. "God will bless you for obeying Him. Let me read something for you." Allegra turned to Malachi 3:10 and read aloud: "'Test me in this,' says the LORD Almighty, 'and see if I will not throw open the floodgates of heaven and pour out so much blessing that you will not have room enough for it.'"

The blessings of God were immediately evident. First, Joan did not have to work anymore and that meant she now had time to attend Allegra's Bible study every week. With every verse she studied, light and understanding dawned.

"Oh, Allegra," Joan effused one day, holding her open Bible, "I just read Proverbs 14:1 where it says, 'The wise woman builds her house, but with her own hands the foolish one tears hers down.' That was *me*. I was that woman." Joan wasn't afraid to admit she had been a fool for ripping apart her marriage, as well as damaging her child.

Which led to the second blessing from God. Because Joan did not have to work, she was able to begin "building her house" by being a stay-at-home mom to Renee. At least, that's what she hoped. John would come home from work and find his wife huddled in a chair with Renee on her lap, reading together and praying. He would scratch his head in bewilderment over this weird but nice change in his wife. "Want to join us?" Joan would ask. But John would only stand there, quiet and aloof as usual. Finally, he would mumble something and head to the den with his things. Joan's eyes would follow him. She struggled to hold the lid on her disappointment. When he turned the corner into the den with not so much as a pleasant "Wow, Joan, I'm glad to see you working so hard to be a good mother," she couldn't hold it in any longer. Her Italian temper erupted.

"Don't you see how hard I'm trying?!" she yelled. "Don't you care?!" Only silence from the den. Pressing her hands to her hot cheeks, she looked down at Renee, cowering on her lap. Plopping her head back against the chair, Joan prayed, *Lord Jesus, forgive me, forgive me. I can't do this on my own. I have no strength. You say in Luke 1:37 that nothing is impossible with You. Please help me put to death my anger. Give me a love for my husband. Please bring him to Your side.*

The next week at Allegra's Bible study, Joan pleaded, "Where do I turn? How can I get rid of this anger? How can I be a good wife and mother?"

Her teacher, with wisdom and a gentle spirit, guided Joan to Proverbs 15:1. "Here's the answer to your first question: 'A gentle answer turns away wrath, but a harsh word stirs up anger.'"

Joan blinked in astonishment. "But how can I do this?" she asked.

Allegra smiled in that wise way again and said, "Don't worry, do not fear. In Psalm 32:8 God says, 'I will instruct you and teach you in the way you should go; I will counsel you and watch over you.'"

Joan went away from that Bible study convinced that it was between her and God. She immediately immersed herself in prayer, rising early in the morning before John and Renee woke up in order to seek the heart of Christ. She travailed in prayer, claiming every Scripture she could, bringing every request with urgent supplication before the throne. She became the woman at midnight knocking on the door of a neighbor to ask for bread . . . she became the woman at the judge's bench, asking time and again for help and mercy. Little did John know that while he softly snored in the next room, his name—and the name of his daughter—was being lifted before the throne room of the God of the universe. And not just one time, or one week, but year after year.

Now, thirty-eight years later, Joan is able to go back to work in data entry, except this time at Joni and Friends. In fact, she's been with our ministry for more than ten years. Her daughters—yes, along the way John and Joan welcomed another little girl into their family, Dawn—have grown into lovely young women who are raising their own children in the Lord and who are encouraging their own husbands who love Christ as they do.

"But . . . but what about your husband?" a visitor who happens to hear Joan's testimony during the office tour will ask.

"What has happened to him?" A wise and knowing smile spreads across Joan's face as she answers, "My husband has yet to come to Christ. But that won't stop me from praying—"

How much richer are obedient lives.

"For *thirty-eight years?*" comes the incredulous question.

"Yes, and for as many years as it takes. I'm simply called to obey. I remarried my husband out of obedience to God knowing full well he was an unbeliever, knowing full well I lacked love for him."

"So nothing has changed?"

"Oh, yes, there's been plenty of change. Maybe not in my husband, but in me."

It is at that point I sit back and admire Joan—the woman who now loves her husband passionately, who now would no more take an extra minute during office break than steal a tube of lipstick. The woman who will remind you if you overpaid sixteen cents on a purchase order. The woman who loves to pray. The woman who loves to obey.

God calls each one of us to obey. Not easy, you say? I know. It never is. In fact, in ourselves it is impossible. But in Christ, nothing is impossible. And that includes the obedience God demands of us. And, oh, how much richer are obedient lives.

Just ask Joan.

My grace is sufficient for you, for my power is made perfect in weakness.

2 CORINTHIANS 12:9

10

YET WILL I TRUST
HIM . . . AND BE STRONG

*T*his chapter is titled "Yet Will I Trust Him . . . and Be Strong," which begs the question of Mary Jane Ponten's life. How do you trust the Lord when, as one person said, "Mary Jane looks like one of those shriveled apple dolls"? How do you trust when kids your own age shun you or—worse yet—are afraid to come near you? How do you trust the Lord when you are rejected by mission boards, and then, when doors finally open to Africa, the Africans take one look at your wild white hair and twisted smile and label you a witch?

At the age of seventy-one, Mary Jane Ponten has faced this and much more. Maybe this is why my friend

MJ, as I like to call her, treasures the truth of 1 Samuel 16:7: "But the LORD said to Samuel, 'Do not consider his appearance or his height, for I have rejected him. The LORD does not look at the things man looks at. Man looks at the outward appearance, but the LORD looks at the heart.'"

Mary Jane is "Mrs. Wheels for the World." Whenever our organization distributes wheelchairs around the world, the trip is always richer when Mary Jane joins the team. But I'm getting ahead of myself. Let's back up a bit.

When Susan and Leo Duggan's baby girl was born back in the summer of 1930, she weighed just four pounds and four ounces. Not much of a start for a newborn back then. "Name her quickly," the doctor told them. "She won't live, and you will need

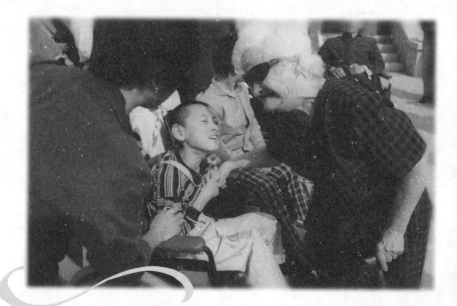

Mary Jane on one of our Wheels for the World trips

a name to put on her death certificate." So they hastily chose a name with no family significance—*Mary Jane.*

Ten days later, tiny Mary Jane was still alive. The doctors shrugged and told her parents to take her home and enjoy her for as long as she lived . . . it wouldn't be long.

"Okay, God, we give her to You," Susan and Leo prayed. "We want our little girl to live, but it's up to You." They claimed Proverbs 3:5–6: "Trust in the LORD with all your heart and lean not on your own understanding; in all your ways acknowledge him, and he will make your paths straight."

When Mary Jane reached the ripe old age of three, the doctors told her parents, "Well, it looks like she will live after all, but she'll never walk, talk, or think. The kindest thing you can do is put this child away in an institution and forget about her."

Fortunately, Susan and Leo didn't take that advice. Instead, claiming God's strength, they went to work. With the help of physical and speech therapists, Susan learned how to work with her daughter at home, and she did so every day. Leo became what Mary Jane likes to call her "social therapist." The requirements for this job were simple but specific—give her lots of love and loads of confidence. It worked. Because of her mother, Mary Jane learned to walk, talk, and think. Because of her father, she also learned to jump rope, roller-skate, ice-skate, and ride a bike.

Not that it came easy. It certainly did not. There were a great many bumps and bruises and a whole lot of worry and anxiety along the way. When Mary Jane was outside doing all those "impossible" things with her dad, her mother stayed in the house and frantically made bread. The kneading helped to quell her fears—stress therapy, you might say. "Of course, I didn't know that back then," MJ told me through her crooked smile. "I thought the fresh baked bread was my reward for trying so hard!"

With years of physical therapy, Mary Jane learned to walk—so well that she was able to wear four-inch heels and still have no noticeable gait. Even after all her therapy her speech isn't perfect, but it is understandable—and it is certainly powerful. Oh, yes . . . can she think? Well, you be the judge. She's had two and a half years of Bible school, and she holds B.A. and M.A. degrees—as well as her Mrs., Mother, and Grandma degrees.

The doctors were wrong on all three counts.

It was in God's strength that, from the beginning of Mary Jane's life, her parents determined: "She is a normal child who just happens to have a physically handicapping condition called cerebral palsy. So what?" It was in His strength that MJ was encouraged to try everything . . . and to pursue excellence in everything she did. And it was in His strength that Susan and Leo applauded and praised each step she made toward every goal.

"I didn't know I couldn't," Mary Jane says, "so I did."

Here's an example: As an eight-year-old, Mary Jane was feeling frustrated that she was still riding a tricycle. "All my friends knew how to ride bicycles," she says, "and I wanted one, too." Of course, no one had bothered to tell her that as a "handicapped child" she should be grateful that she could even ride a trike. No one suggested that a two-wheeler was way too dangerous for a child "like her." So what did Mary Jane ask for that Christmas? A bike, of course.

And that's what she got—a two-wheeled bicycle. Mary Jane was so excited she could hardly stand it. "I took that bike and walked it right over to my friend Elsie's house, half a block away," she told me. (And there is still more than a little pride in her voice.) "It didn't matter one bit that I couldn't ride it yet. Santa had enough confidence in me to bring me a two-wheeler, so who was I to doubt?"

Then the work began, and this was back in the dark ages, before training wheels were invented. "Every pleasant evening that spring, Daddy took me across Seventy-first Street to a stretch of sidewalk along Oakwood Cemetery and we would ride my bike. Daddy held tight to help me get the feel of balancing. He would let go for brief moments. Those moments gradually became longer and longer until all of a sudden one day I was riding. I went a whole block before I knew I was alone. What a feeling! I could ride my bike. It was so great."

It's a shock to come face-to-face with our own weakness.

When she was in fourth grade, Mary Jane was kicked out of her neighborhood school. Being disabled, she just couldn't meet the teacher's expectations. Her physical body was not up to it.

"Dear Lord, give us Your strength," her parents prayed as they enrolled their daughter in Samuel Gompers School for exceptional children on the South Side of Chicago. The entire school, from preschool through eighth grade, was conducted for physically disabled children.

"How well I remember walking into that fourth-grade room," says Mary Jane. "Up till then I knew I had been born with 'spastic paralysis'—that's what they called it back then. Now they call it cerebral palsy. But I thought that room was pathetic. All those crippled children sitting in the desks, some even in wheelchairs."

Mary Jane stubbornly determined, "I don't belong here! I'm not like that!" Because the transfer had been arranged by her doctor, she figured she would stay until the mistake could be straightened out. If that didn't happen soon, well . . . she would just have to prove she didn't belong there.

"Until that day," MJ told me, "I really didn't know I was handicapped."

It's a shock to come face-to-face with our own weakness, isn't it?

Mary Jane continued in that particular system through the twelfth grade. She could no longer deny that she was disabled. But even as she became aware of her weakness, she was being pointed toward the strength of Jesus Christ.

It was in that weakness that MJ began to hone the wonderful sense of humor that keeps everyone around her laughing. "Life is too short to be so serious that one misses the richness of humor," she insists. "That's true of anyone. But I think it is more true of someone like me who looks, talks, or acts physically out of the ordinary."

It must have taken more than humor to learn to drive on the streets of Chicago in a shift-on-the-floor '38 Ford! But all her friends were getting their learner's permits the day they were old enough to qualify, and Mary Jane wanted hers, too. She got it, and her father taught her to drive. "Dad owned the car, so he set the standards for driving it. I did it Daddy's way, but I did it."

Mary Jane's parents taught their daughter to set her own personal goals and then to work steadily toward achieving them.

"When I went off to college I was still holding a glass or cup with both hands. It was embarrassing." So MJ set herself a goal of learning to drink with one hand. It had nothing to do with the law of gravity, like learning to ride the bike. It had nothing to do with her parents' rules, like learning to drive the car. No, this was a personal goal, one she set for herself.

One of Mary Jane's personal goals was to walk the way everyone else did. She reached that goal. Another was to speak perfectly. That goal she didn't reach. But she has no regrets about having set it. "Without it, I'd hate to say how bad my speech would be today."

Like Mary Jane, I have learned to set my goals high enough to force myself to stretch, sometimes painfully. I can't always reach my goals either, but at least I've tried . . . and I'm better off for that. MJ has good advice about personal goals. "They are things you have control over," she says. "Set them wisely."

As MJ was growing up, church was always at the center of her activities, so it was natural for her to respond early to a call to missionary service. "From the time I was twelve years old, I knew I was going to be a missionary to China. I had been called. I had said yes. As far as I was concerned, there was no further discussion."

But while she was at Northwestern Bible School, a surprising thing happened. God took hold of her heart and showed her that what she had mistaken for her own strength was really God's strength. What she had mistaken for a settled-in-heaven personal relationship with Him was actually just a relationship by association. She was preparing to serve the Lord and she didn't even really know Him! "Until then I just assumed I was a Christian. Hadn't I received the very highest calling, that of a missionary? And hadn't I accepted it?"

For an entire week she struggled with the question of where she stood with God. Finally on Friday, during chapel, the matter was settled forever in heaven and on earth. "I gave my heart to Jesus and He received it. And never for a moment from then till now have I questioned my relationship with Him."

But God was still developing Mary Jane. "During my last year of college, I finally got it through my thick skull that no reputable mission board would send someone with cerebral palsy to China—or to anywhere else as a missionary. And I certainly would never go out under a less than reputable mission board."

So it was all for nothing?

Not at all. God had used Mary Jane's desire and determination to get her to work hard in high school and college and to get the best education she possibly could. If there was never to be anything more, the goal had been worth that.

For two years MJ corresponded with Bud Ponten, a fellow Christian who also had been born with cerebral palsy. Their correspondence matured into friendship, and their friendship into love. She and Bud were married in 1962, and they were blessed with two children. Their life together was truly a gift from God, and they were able to work together in His service in Colorado.

When God called Mary Jane's beloved husband home to be with Him, Mary Jane reviewed her life. More than once during her sixty-one years she had asked God to heal her. Each time He had said, "No, Mary Jane. I have better plans for you."

Once again she turned in her Bible to 2 Corinthians 12 and read about the apostle Paul who had struggled with his own limitations. What was it that hindered him? A problem with his eyesight? Bad hearing? A painful limp? Maybe he had a slight case of cerebral palsy. The specific diagnosis must not be important because we're never told what it was. What we are told is that *three times* he pleaded with God to take the infirmity away from him. But God didn't. Instead, He told Paul, "My grace is sufficient for you, for my power is made perfect in weakness" (v. 9). And how did Paul respond? He wrote: "Therefore I will boast all the more gladly about my weaknesses, so that Christ's power may rest on me. This is why, for Christ's sake, I delight in weaknesses, in insults, in hardships, in persecutions, in difficulties. For when I am weak, then I am strong" (vv. 9–10).

"Well then," MJ decided, "I had better delight in my weakness . . . and in my hardships . . . and in my difficulties. Because I know I am weak, and I so want to be strong!"

For many years Mary Jane had served on the board of directors for the Cerebral Palsy Association in her area. When John Nix joined the board, he told Mary Jane about his twin girls, both affected with CP. They discovered their mutual love for Jesus Christ and their concerns about the church's attitude toward people with disabilities. Still, Mary Jane's first reaction was: *Get over it. That's just the way things are. Get on with life.*

As Mary Jane and John continued to share over lots of pie and coffee, God nudged her: *Remember how it felt when others in the body of Christ whispered about you and refused to let you do things because they had determined you couldn't . . . and slapped labels on you and all the rest? Remember how you learned to overlook all that? Remember how I gave you My strength to do it?* That's when God began to change Mary Jane's heart. John was right. There was a need for the church—the body of Christ—to genuinely accept people with disabilities, to actively reach out to win them, and then to nurture them in their spiritual lives. Right there, sitting in the coffee shop at the Village Inn, Mary Jane Ponten and John Nix dared to share a dream. And Mephibosheth Ministry was born.

It may seem as though it was a new beginning for MJ, but it wasn't really. She recognizes that. "It seems that God has been preparing me for this ministry all along. Step-by-step He has allowed circumstances to get me ready for this portion of my life."

Mary Jane can't help but chuckle when she remembers her long-ago realization that, because of her disability, no reputable mission board would ever send her to China. Guess what! In the year 2000 she went to China as a short-term missionary, not in *spite* of her disability, but *because* of it. And that's not all. She has been overseas with Wheels for the World so many times that last year extra pages had to be added to her passport.

Can't you just hear God laughing along with her?

Mary Jane's job with us is to train pastors and church leaders to reach out to disabled people in their communities, to accept them with dignity, and to effectively share God's love with them. She also trains them in evangelism techniques and instructs them in training their church members to accept these "outcasts of society."

I love MJ's commitment, and I love her attitude. She always says, "No one has ever been able to convince me that I am handicapped. I have a physically handicapping condition called cerebral palsy. I look funny. I walk just a bit off-beat. I talk really weird. Fortunately my mind has not been affected. But do these circumstances make me a handicapped person? Some would say yes. I beg to differ."

And that's not just a matter of semantics. The *disabled person* thinks first about the disability and second about the person. It becomes a matter of course to say, "I can't do this because I'm disabled." But the well-adjusted person faces a circumstance head-on—if there's a barrier involved that can't be overcome, then and only then does he or she contemplate the disability.

"I am not so wrapped up in my handicap that it is the first thing on my mind," Mary Jane explains. "I am a normal person with many interests. First of all I am a *person*, a human being. I just happen to have CP." Then she adds, "Once we have accepted who we are, we can take the next step of adjusting to our life and lifestyle."

People look at Mary Jane and see someone who has succeeded "in the real world"—at school, in college, in the workplace, and as a wife and mother. "She's too positive!" they say. "She isn't telling the whole story."

MJ doesn't see it that way. "I've spent my life outgrowing, overcoming, and overpowering all those negatives."

And she certainly is not immune to them even now, even after seventy-one years. Not long ago she was at the gas station filling her tank when two teenage girls came up behind her. As she removed the nozzle, one said in a voice she couldn't possibly miss, "People like that shouldn't be let out on the street." What shocked Mary Jane wasn't what the girls said. It was the anger it still stirred up in her.

No, even now it is not easy sailing for Mary Jane. It never will be. Not even among God's people, where love and acceptance are to be the strongest. "I've walked into churches where people look at me and treat me like an idiot. Then they find out I'm the speaker, and suddenly everyone is quiet. Uh . . . oh!"

When Mary Jane looks honestly at herself, she is well aware that in herself she is weak. She recognizes it and she accepts it. It is a fact of her life, and rejecting it or ignoring it will not make it go away. In her own strength, she knows what she would be . . . a bitter old lady. But, oh, what she is doing through Christ's strength!

"I am writing a lot now, most of it for the mentally challenged population—the very group I abhorred as a child and ran away from most of my life. And I love it! Doesn't God have an absolutely marvelous sense of humor?"

He certainly does.

Several weeks ago, Mary Jane traveled with John Wern and the Wheels for the World team to Cuba to begin laying the groundwork for helping evangelicals in this Communist country develop a disability ministry. On one sunny afternoon, their small group was standing on a sidewalk in downtown Santiago de Cuba.

Two preteen Cuban girls walked by and when they saw Mary Jane, their eyes bulged. They stopped, huddled together, and simply kept staring. Since Mary Jane is now a veteran at dealing with other people's awkward curiosity, she smiled. The girls did not smile back. Instead, they inched closer until one of them was less than three feet away from Mary Jane's face. The preteener cocked her head and twisted her face into a funny expression that communicated, *Eewww . . . I've never seen such an oddity as this!* In fact, the girl was downright rude. As a grandmother, Mary Jane's reaction was to wag her finger and scold the girl for being so impolite.

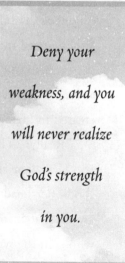

Deny your weakness, and you will never realize God's strength in you.

"I wanted to smack the girl," Mary Jane told me later. But

instead, through the translator who was standing next to her, Mary Jane said, "It's okay to be curious, and I welcome any questions you want to ask. Actually, I love young people like you. I have five grandchildren of my own!" The two girls softened a bit, and then Mary Jane invited them to shake her hand. They shyly reached out, and they left with a change of heart.

"*That*," MJ said, turning to her translator, "was disability ministry in action."

My friend used that week in Cuba to forge new friendships and teach new concepts to pagans and Christians alike. At one teaching session, a young, mildly disabled woman leaned forward in her seat, listening intently to Mary Jane talk about the biblical origin of disability. Later on, the woman told my friend, "My father cursed me after I was born. I always thought his curse was the cause of my handicap," to which MJ replied, "Ah, take a look at Psalm 139. God knew you before you were born, and you were created in His image."

"Really?" The woman was amazed. "Not because of a curse?"

Mary Jane smiled in that wonderfully unique way of hers and shook her head. "There's no curse. Taboos and hexes and curses are no match for God, for 'Greater is He who is in you, than he who is in the world.'"

In the face of stares and strange looks, Mary Jane says, "Yet will I trust Him." Call her a witch, a scary old lady, or a "retard" and MJ will smile and say, "Yet will I trust Him." What's more, she'll say, "You should trust Him, too!"

In one way or another, every one of us is disabled. Oh, you

may not look like it as MJ does. You may be completely able-bodied and very accomplished. But don't be fooled. If you are operating on your own, you are operating out of weakness. Deny this weakness, and you will never realize God's strength in you.

Mary Jane Ponten speaks with the strength of Christ. And that's why she's traveling the world. It's the message she shares with everyone she meets.

You were bought at a price;

do not become slaves of men.

❧

1 CORINTHIANS 7:23

11

YET WILL I TRUST
HIM . . . AND BE FREE

On Sunday morning at our little church, you can always find Ken and me sitting on the left aisle, four rows from the front, next to Dave and Patti Guth. We feel a kinship with the Guths. It's easy because Dave and Patti are, well . . . downright likable. You couldn't find a more competent and caring church elder than Dave. He's wise and thoughtful, always handling God's Word with reverence and respect, being careful not to take anything out of context. He's compassionate, always looking out for the underdog or newcomers at church. Most of all, he's forthright in a considerate way and as honest as the day is long.

Ken and I learned that about Dave when he and his small construction team remodeled our bedroom. Every morning, right on time, big, burly Dave, wearing plaid shirt, jeans, and carpenter's suspenders, was on the job. And no aspect of the job was beneath him—if a plastic covering on a window blew out at

Dave and Patti Guth

night, it was nothing for Dave to get in his truck and come on over to fix it. Every two-by-four and box of tile was accounted for, and if there was even a slight chance we might go over budget or his estimates, he was quick to alert us. Every nail was driven solidly and every bolt tightened well. This man is not the kind to cut corners or fudge a project.

Considering what Dave came through, that's saying something.

Not that the little farming community of Mokena, Illinois, back in the early sixties didn't give him a good start. It blessed him with broad midwestern horizons, cornfields to wander through, and creeks to fish in. Mokena had a Boy Scout troop in which thirteen-year-old Dave earned his Christian service merit badge. He grew up under a kind but exacting father from whom he learned all his carpentry skills. Dave's father not only built homes, he also strove to build Christian character in his son.

He had no idea how much Dave needed it. At the age of fifteen, Dave had begun to mess around with the wrong crowd, tuning into Jimi Hendrix and sitting around campfires with his buddies, experimenting with marijuana. Thankfully, Dave still attended Sunday services with his folks. He occasionally helped his dad on fix-it jobs around the church grounds and went to the youth group when something special was going on. Deep in his heart, Dave was still the Boy Scout, and with his conscience still tender, he invited Christ into his life.

What a difference Jesus made! Dave felt free to say no to his old friends and yes to the kids at church. The first thing he did was to start meeting with a few Christian buddies after school to pray for their fellow students. His dad couldn't have been more proud. And the son couldn't have been happier. At least, at first.

The late sixties brought change. Even to Mokena with its tree-lined roads, main street stores, and the surrounding farms and fields. The winds of change were felt most forcefully in the hallways of Lincoln Way High School. "Hey, we're free! Free to do our own thing!" was everyone's cry. The boys' bathroom became a smoky haven for kids cutting class, and there was always a car or two in the parking lot where marijuana could be bought or sold. Radios blasted the Beatles. Girls' skirts got shorter and their sweaters got tighter. However, when the Rolling Stones would sing, "I Can't Get No Satisfaction," Dave knew better. He felt free enough in Christ.

Besides, he preferred the company of the kids at church. Especially one girl who came regularly to the youth group. He found himself sidling up to her often with Coke and pizza in hand. After that, it was sitting next to her and praying together. Then, holding hands and taking her home after Sunday evening services. When he'd park his car outside her house and reach for her hand to pray, Dave hardly realized he was speaking less to his Lord, and more for the listening pleasure of his girlfriend. She became, in fact, the focus of his faith. Before long, he found himself trading the satisfaction he had found in Christ for the sexual satisfaction he could find in the backseat of his car.

He tried to fight the enticements of the flesh, but his passions prevailed. After high school graduation and at nineteen years of age, Dave and his girlfriend married. As they walked back down the aisle, hoping he could legitimize his illegitimate relationship, he firmly gripped the hand of his new bride. *This must work,* he insisted. But all hopes for a textbook marriage ended when they arrived home from the honeymoon and closed the apartment door behind them. Marriage became one sickening disappointment after another.

Dave was desperate to medicate his emotional pain. It started when one of his old friends with whom he used to dabble in pot called one night. "Hey, Dave, wanna hang out tonight?"

Why not? he thought. *I've already ruined my life, my marriage . . . my Christian testimony. What the heck! Why not smoke a joint?* A few hours later he was over at his friend's house, rolling marijuana. He held the joint up, lit it, and watched a trail of smoke snake slowly upward. He put it to his lips and drew deeply.

> *The fire of addiction* must *be fought with the fire of the pleasures God offers.*

While Dave was doing his thing, his wife was out doing her thing. Two years later, the marriage crashed and, with it, any hopes of a happy life on a tree-lined street in Mokena.

That's it! Dave thought. *Lord, I tried it Your way, and it didn't work. Now I'm going to do it my way.* The next few years were a blur of barhopping, downing a few drinks, talking about nothing, walking out to the parking lot to smoke a joint with his buddies, and then back to the bar for more drinks until 2:00 A.M. If he wasn't with his friends, Dave would get high back at his apartment, smoking and **flipping** through his collection of pornographic magazines. "Kicks just keep getting harder to find," as the seventies anthem went. The flicker of lust's pleasures inflamed into a hot and consuming greed for even more pot and more pornography.

One morning when Dave was at his father's shop sipping a cup of coffee to ease his headache, his dad walked up to him, put down his tools, and placed his hand on his son's shoulder. Dave looked up through swollen red eyes. For a long, quiet moment father and son held each other's gaze. His dad spoke first. "I don't know what's going on, Dave, but I know you're not walking with the Lord. Son, I was there when you accepted Christ. I saw the difference it made. I only want to say one thing. You were bought with a price."

It was a verse Dave had memorized by heart years ago. But now, it cut deep. Thing was, his father forgot the second half of 1 Corinthians 7:23: "You were bought at a price; *do not become slaves of men*" (emphasis added). The conviction of sin was bitter. He knew he was a slave to drugs and pornography. But that afternoon, whatever conviction he felt earlier was doused by his desire—his need—to get high. He was back to his pot and porno magazines.

The late seventies brought more changes to Mokena. It was not the small town it used to be. Dave wasn't the same either. He was not the same kid who used to pray for his classmates. Far from it. So far that he pulled up roots and headed to California to work for a contractor near Los Angeles. Settling into a new area meant hunting up an apartment, finding business contacts, and doing banking. At one of those banks he met a woman who would change his life.

Her name was Patti, and not only did she help him open his account, but she was about the most pleasant person he had met since moving to California. They struck up a quick friendship. Something was different about Patti. Clear blue eyes, a ready smile, a natural inclination to simply ask questions and listen, an ability to look on the bright side—and someone who seemed to *fit* with him.

"Hey, how about dinner this weekend?" Dave would ask.

"Sure," she said happily. They would find a corner table at a restaurant and over a bottle of wine, they would have fun talking. Patti began to trust this new friend and, before long, she divulged that she had recently gone through a divorce. They'd finish off their bottle of wine, order another, and share more.

It didn't take much to push them to live together. Six months later, out of convenience and compatibility, they both signed on a home—Dave was glad that he could begin to build equity, and Patti could be there to watch the house while Dave was out of town working. She could drink and he could use drugs . . . and neither would care, neither talked about the other's habits. Indeed, they did *fit* with one another and deep affection was even growing. A year and a half later, they married.

Patti thought nothing when Dave began growing a small plot of marijuana in the backyard. Dave thought nothing if, when they were planning a drive, Patti would fill a thermos full of wine to take with her. They felt free to do their own thing. Besides, they weren't party people—they preferred getting high at home.

Dave and Patti never realized their lives were spiraling downward at a breakneck speed. One night, however, something happened that would spark the beginning of a change for Dave. He and a friend, with whom they'd had dinner earlier, were rolling joints on the coffee table, laughing it up and getting high. At the same time, Patti was starting on her fourth glass of wine. She came shuffling into the living room, a little unstable on her feet. Dave noticed her eyelids were half-open and although she tried to share in the conversation, her words were a little slurred and incoherent. She mumbled something else and then went back into the other room.

Dave's friend shook his head in contempt. He pulled on his joint and said in a haze of smoke, "Hey, man, your wife really has a problem." The snide comment stung Dave. He loved Patti more than anything. He jumped to her defense and challenged, "Look, guy, what do you think *we're* doing? Maybe we're the ones with the problem!"

That thought, like a prickly burr, wouldn't let him rest. His buddies were beginning to move on to harder drugs, yet he could not bring himself to go that route. He would wake up in the morning, look in the mirror, and insist, "Today I am not going to use!" But fifteen minutes later, he was rolling another joint. The next morning he would slam his fist on the sink. *I am pathetic! Absolutely pathetic!*

To keep from heading down the path of his friends who were now using cocaine, Dave knew he would have to "white knuckle" it. Without hesitating, he headed to the kitchen, pulled out the trash bag full of marijuana he had been collecting, and proceeded to burn the drug in the fireplace, along with all his pipes and papers.

Shortly thereafter, Patti also was to come face-to-face with her own addiction. Her bank manager walked up with a handful of papers and asked, "Patti, what is going on? Your work is really suffering lately. Can you tell me what is wrong?"

Patti hardly hesitated. "I'm an alcoholic."

Her manager put down the papers and said softly, "I'm glad you told me. Now we can do something about it."

The next thirty days were spent in a care unit, participating in Alcoholics Anonymous meetings. Patti was able to tell how, as a little girl, her parents would offer her sips from their glasses of manhattans. She described how, years later, she would hide bottles of vodka and wine under her bed or in the closet. She talked about how she would sleep till noon on days off and about the increasing number of blackouts she had been experiencing. And she shared how grateful she was to her husband, Dave—he had now placed himself in a twelve-step program, too.

The counselor at the care unit described how important it was to have a Higher Authority to go to. Patti had been raised in Catholic schools and knew that, for her, God was probably that Higher Power. Yet she felt unmoved to do anything about it. The idea of God was tainted by her distaste for organized religion. Yet one day when the counselor played the hymn "Amazing Grace" on the cassette player, she felt a knot in her throat. Patti knew something was missing in her life.

Dave knew it, too. He used to enjoy working in his garage on weekends and would always see his neighbors across the street pile into their car to go to church on Sundays. However, lately he had been feeling that same knot in his throat—just weeks earlier during one of his twelve-step meetings, Dave had acknowledged God as his Higher Power.

The next Sunday he did something completely out of the

ordinary. When he saw his neighbors come out of the house, all dressed for Sunday school, he crossed the street, shared a few greetings, and asked, "Mind if I go to church with you next week?" The husband and wife looked at each other, smiled, and said, "Not at all," shaking Dave's hand.

Over the next few Sundays at church, a hundred Bible verses came flooding back to Dave's memory, encouraging and convicting him with every sermon, hymn, and turn of the page in Scripture. One verse was Galatians 5:1: "It is for freedom that Christ has set us free. Stand firm, then, and do not let yourselves be burdened again by a yoke of slavery."

That morning when he came home from church, Dave dropped to his knees and prayed, *Oh, God, I am Your prodigal son. I ran away from You and squandered everything You gave me. But now I am back and I want to repent. I want to be completely free in You to say no to drugs.* He got up feeling as though an enormous weight had been lifted off him.

At first, Patti treated Dave's conversion with disdain. "Why do you have to go to church?" she would say. "Good grief, you don't get home until noon!" Yet something still wasn't quite right. Inside she still felt restless and itchy. Patti had to admit that she wasn't comfortable in her sobriety—the emptiness that used to be filled by alcohol was still there.

Six months passed—half a year since Dave had come to Christ. Six months for Patti to see what Jesus could do in a person's life. Patti could not bear the restlessness any longer. One Saturday night she approached Dave and said, "I think I would like to go to church with you." Not long after that, Patti placed her life in the hands of her Savior, Jesus Christ. For the very first time, Patti and Dave knew the truth about themselves, about each other, and, most important, about the Lord. As Jesus says in John 8:32, "You will know the truth, and the truth will set you free."

One day, long after she was sober, Patti discovered a new dimension of her addiction. Since giving up drinking, she had developed a preference for chocolate. That afternoon, as she was driving home from work, Patti found herself wondering, *Hmmm . . . do I have enough M&M's at home to last me tonight in front of the TV? Maybe I should stop and get some. And perhaps an extra bag for tomorrow.* She almost slammed on the brakes. She was virtually at the same stoplight on the same bridge where she used to wonder if she had enough wine at the house! It struck her that her body still craved the enormous amounts of sugar from wine; she had simply traded one addiction for another.

The Guths realized that their new life in Christ was going to be a long process of sanctification. A process of taking one day at a time, abiding in His Word, and choosing to obey Him every morning, noon, and night. Their lives were to be a daily repetition of Titus 2:11–12: "For the grace of God that brings salvation . . . teaches us to say 'No' to ungodliness and worldly passions, and to live self-controlled, upright and godly lives in this present age."

Fifteen years have passed. If you were to ask the Guths about their favorite Bible verse, they would repeat 2 Peter 1:5–7: "Make every effort to add to your faith goodness; and to goodness, knowledge; and to knowledge, self-control; and to self-control, perseverance; and to perseverance, godliness; and to godliness, brotherly kindness; and to brotherly kindness, love." For them, it's worth the effort to wake up every day at five in the morning so they can spend half an hour together "adding to their faith" by praying and reading from the Word.

> *The fight to remain free in Christ is the fight to stay utterly satisfied with God.*

Dave and Patti will be the first to say that the fire of addiction cannot be doused by threats, warnings, or attempts to turn over new leaves. The fire of addiction *must* be fought with the fire of the pleasures God offers. One must fight the pull of earthly pleasures with the massive promises of superior happiness in the Lord. As Dr. John Piper has said, "We must swallow up the flicker of lust's [and addiction's] pleasure in the conflagration of holy satisfaction." God must be our aim. The fight to remain free in Christ is the fight to stay utterly satisfied with God.

Dave often thinks back to the time when his father took a risk, intruding and reminding Dave he had been bought with a price. "My father did not know how his little comment would ultimately turn me around," Dave says. "It's a reminder that God will use our smallest encouragements to get someone back on course."

Patti, bless her heart, finds time in between her duties as church treasurer and custom art framer to get me up in my wheelchair three mornings a week. We always sing a hymn and pray as she stands next to me in the garage before I head to work. We pray for our husbands. We say time and again how we would be wallowing in sin were it not for the grace of God. We rehearse how much we need Christ. We remark on the marvelous handiwork of His creation in my front yard, with marigolds blooming, blue skies above, and pine branches bobbing in the breeze. We sigh deeply and smile at each other. Once in a while, before parting, I will ask her, "Shall we sing your favorite hymn?"

It's the same hymn that Patti and Dave and Ken and I often sing at church.

> Amazing grace! how sweet the sound—
> That saved a wretch like me!
> I once was lost but now am found,
> Was blind but now I see.

They once were slaves to sin and to drugs . . . but thanks to Christ, they're *free*.

By this all men will know
that you are my disciples,
if you love one another.

❧

JOHN 13:35

12

YET WILL I TRUST
HIM . . . AND LOVE

*Y*ou'd have to go far to find a more beautiful
dawn break across a horizon than in the north-
east corner of Texas. In early June, the morning mist
rises off the Red River and paints the pastures and woods
in a soft pearlescent glow. The fireflies fade into the forest just as the trees begin to echo with the chatter of a
thousand happy birds. Roosters crow from farms beyond
the river, and the smell of new mown hay with a hint of
honeysuckle freshens the air. Such a morning might call
you down to the creek to sit on the bank, hug your
knees, and watch the perch break the calm of the water
to get gnats. Or maybe your mama would send you to

Billy Burnett at age 12

hunt up eggs for frying or fresh milk for making grits. If you were blessed enough for it to be a Saturday morning, you could play catch in the woods with a friend or maybe catch crayfish—Mama could boil them up with salt, spices, and crushed tomatoes and have them tasting as good as any lobster.

With all this, Billy Burnett believed he was as rich as any boy in town. The boys in his hometown of Texarkana would have said differently. Nobody ever heard of rich black folks in that corner of Texas. Especially in the late forties. Billy's people were poor. They had moved to Texarkana from the little town of Hooks, thirty miles southwest. Back in Hooks, Billy was just the eleventh child of twelve born to sharecroppers living in that small cabin on the corner of Jimmy Lynch's farm. It had no heat, no running water, and no electricity.

Then again, the house in Texarkana didn't have running water or heat either. Billy's dad had built their home with his own two hands. Willie—that was his dad's name—was glad they had left their sharecropping life behind, but that didn't mean life was any easier. Willie worked hard to provide for his family, whether butchering at the slaughterhouse, operating the machines at the town sawmill, or doing carpentry. Yes, the house was a big step up from a sharecropper's cabin, but to five-year-old Billy, it didn't matter where he lived—just so long as he could catch fireflies, fish for perch, and play in the woods.

Billy's home in Texarkana was backed up against large woods, thick with squirrel and rabbit. There was a pump out back, as well as an outhouse. There was also enough acreage for chickens and for growing sweet potatoes, carrots, and corn. There was good hunting, too. His father would come in from the forest with his rifle in one hand and a couple of squirrels slung over his shoulder. That night they'd have pan-fried squirrel, salted and peppered with gravy, biscuits, and sweet potatoes. Life felt good.

But it was a struggle. Especially with such a large family. Billy often took his father hot meals to the sawmill at lunchtime. Mama Teal—that's what everybody called Billy's mother—had to be at home to tend to her brood, but she squeezed in domestic work in the homes of white folks to help make ends meet. Billy would sit on the back steps and watch his mama, with her hair covered in an orange-and-black hand-wrapped turban, leaning over the wash bucket, scrubbing clothes in rhythm to a song she'd be humming. His mother may have been a hard worker, but to him she seemed to possess a grace and gentle beauty reserved for town dignitaries. He loved her dearly.

When it came time to harvest cotton in the spring and fall, Mama Teal, with whichever of her children could help, would make extra money for the family by picking cotton. Eight-year-old Billy was too young to go to the fields, and he longed for the day when he could join his mother and sisters. "Oh, Mama, can I go to pick cotton? Please?!" he would implore.

Early that same fall, he would have his chance.

"Time to get up, baby." His mama stirred him from his sleep. Billy dressed himself in his worn overalls and a plaid shirt. He shoved a hunter's cap on his head and ran out the door. The sun had not quite broken through the darkness, and Billy tied his earflaps tightly under his chin. He tugged at his mother's dress and asked excitedly, "When's the truck comin' to pick us up? Do I get to pick cotton today?"

His mother, knowing very well the hard labor that lay ahead, and feeling the weight of facing another day in the fields, leaned down and pulled Billy close to ease the chill. "Yes, Billy," she said wistfully, "the truck will be here soon and, yes, baby, you'll get to pick cotton."

It was the first of many mornings in the field. Even though he was a child, Billy worked up to ten hours a day to try to fill his sack. He scrambled to keep up with larger and stronger men who could earn $2.50 a day picking a hundred pounds of cotton. Billy would bring home only fifty cents, but that was okay. That fifty cents was needed. And so, the routine continued. The truck would stop at the edge of the field in the early morning and unload the workers who would get their sacks from the field boss. The workers would spread out among the rows and begin picking, walking, stooping, and stretching, row after row. The sun would rise higher in the sky, evaporating the cool of the morning. For Billy, the novelty of working in the fields also evaporated.

The sweetness of Billy's childhood, the carefree abandon of racing across a field to catch fireflies, or of fishing in the creek, all the tender innocence of adolescence abruptly ended one late afternoon in the summer of 1958. The sun was high and hot, and the humid air hissed with the sound of bugs. Twelve-year-old Billy was bent over and chopping, a process that thinned the cotton plants. He stood to stretch his tired back for a moment and stared at the older men and women who, in the waves of heat, shimmered like ghosts in a mirage. Suddenly, he was seized with fright. *Oh, Lord, will I have to do this forever? Is there no hope for me?* The next instant, he heard King Davis, the large, burly field boss, shout, "Get back to work, boy!"

The twelve-year-old went home that day feeling old.

However, there were other changes in the summer of 1958. Good ones. It was at vacation Bible school that Cousin Bessie, a large, happy-spirited, Christian woman, led Billy to the Lord. Billy loved the Christian life! Back home, he even hammered a little makeshift lectern and forced his sister to listen to his sermons. No one was more proud than his parents, Willie and Mama Teal.

"Bill, now you know those folks who let their dogs out on you when you walk to school?" his dad would say.

Billy nodded.

"Now you be sure to *love* those people. You've got to love 'em like the Lord loves them, you hear?"

Billy nodded again. New things were expected of him—from his parents and from his God.

In the summer of 1960, the test of Billy's Christian character, as well as his education about real life in the South, would begin in earnest. He was fourteen years old, tossing hides in a slaughterhouse, and dreading another summer in the cotton fields. His brother-in-law told him about an opening for a busboy/dishwasher at The Embers, a whites-only restaurant. He got the job. The hours were long and the pay was minimal, but Billy considered it a step up.

Sixteen-year-old Billy and his dad

For the most part, he learned to ignore the racial slurs that other kids would hurl at him from their cars when he had to walk through white neighborhoods on the way to work. Occasionally, he was pelted with a beer can. And one time, someone sicced a Doberman pinscher on him—he was scraped badly after having to race through thick hedges to escape the snapping dog. All the while, he kept his composure, thinking of the words of his father: "Billy, you give these people the love of Jesus. They hurled insults at Him . . . they'll hurl them at you."

Billy told himself this when a male waiter would throw things at him or the kitchen manager would drop food just so Billy would have to clean up the mess. Working in an air-conditioned restaurant was a lot better than working in the fields. Sometimes patrons would give him tips by tossing the money on the floor, just so he'd remember his place. Billy learned to live with the comments of one diner who came to The Embers every Friday night. After a drink or two, the man would always ask, "Have you been a good nigger today?" to which young Billy would reply, "Yes, sir," which in turn would provoke a nasty, "Don't you get smart with me, boy!"

He never mentioned these things to his parents.

One night after a particularly busy shift, Billy's work crew was preparing to leave when a discussion grew loud regarding the pay owed to one of the cooks. One of the diners nearby picked up a Coke bottle and threw it. It crashed against Billy's head, breaking into a hundred pieces and laying open his scalp.

"Get out of here!" the man shouted.

Billy's head was bleeding badly. He was hauled off to a little clinic in a black neighborhood where he was stitched up and sent home with glass still in his scalp. When he was dropped off, still reeling from a concussion, his father and mother embraced him hard. With a choke in his throat, Billy's dad just repeated,

"Vengeance belongs to the Lord, son. Hating is not the answer. All white people aren't bad just like all black people aren't good. Vengeance belongs to the Lord."

Billy tried hard to remember his father's advice. That wasn't easy during the summer of 1962 when the South was embroiled in the civil rights struggle. Texarkana was no longer the sleepy little town bordered by forests to play in and streams to fish in. Sixteen-year-old Bill was tired of the constant disparaging remarks, doors slammed in his face, the demeaning treatment. Without giving it much thought, Billy joined two of his high school friends at a sit-in at a local diner.

The next day there was a photo and an article in the Texarkana paper. The owner of the diner recognized Billy as one of the night-shift workers at The Embers. Within forty-eight hours, two white police officers showed up at the restaurant and took Billy to a storage room.

"Are you a good nigger?" one of them asked.

Billy was shaking, and he quietly replied in a submissive tone, "Yes, yes, I am." The other officer placed a service revolver against Billy's temple and said, "Then don't you *ever* let me see you—"

Billy was certain he was going to die that night. But when they shoved him out of the storage room, he realized he wasn't going to lose his life. Just his job. And the next job after that. And the next one. God was looking out for Billy, though, because he ended up with a great job at a local hotel working for more pay than ever.

Still, those were hard days. Little wonder that after high school graduation Billy decided to move to California to live with his sister and her family. It was difficult to leave his folks in Texas, but he loved being with his sister's family and attending their little Baptist church at the end of the street. Things looked so much brighter and better in California. He met and married his wife, Shirley, at the Baptist church. He was discipled by his pastor and shortly thereafter became a deacon, following in the steps of his father, who was a deacon and a Sunday school teacher. The next years were filled with some of the sweetest, most memorable times of family fun and Christian fellowship in that wonderful neighborhood.

When Billy was twenty-one years old, he was picked for a training program in the aerospace industry. Realizing that he

Billy and me

would never progress further without more education, and knowing he had to provide for his wife and baby daughter, Billy, at the age of twenty-seven, began attending college at night while working full-time. He graduated summa cum laude with an AA degree. From there, he enrolled in Cal State University at Dominguez Hills and graduated magna cum laude as one of the first students to receive the Industrial Management degree, also receiving the highest award for excellence in the program. A week after his graduation, Billy and Shirley were blessed with a second child, their son, Byron.

In 1982, Billy became the first African-American engineering manager to work at Colt Industries. When the company went through major upheaval and had millions of dollars tied up in nonfunctioning equipment, Billy assumed responsibility for that equipment and, with the application of high-tech innovation, had things fully functional and generating profits for the company within a year. He was rewarded with full tuition to Pepperdine University's Executive MBA program, which he completed in 1987.

But by 1986, the community in which Billy and his young family lived was changing drastically. After their home was burglarized three times in one year, the Burnetts moved to Newbury Park, California, in order to protect their children from the influence of gangs and drugs. They attended a church of twelve hundred people and, within three years, Billy was asked by Dale Evrist, the teaching pastor, to join the church's staff as executive pastor. After seven years of overseeing the church's administration,

Billy responded to Joni and Friends' need for a vice president of administration. He began work with our ministry in 1997.

From the first day that this happy, broad-shouldered, tall African-American man sat at his desk, I could tell Billy was going to enjoy working at Joni and Friends. Right away, he set about helping to secure the infrastructure of our organization, pouring all his talent and expertise into streamlining our budget process. I felt that Billy had found a home with us. One day in 1998, however, he came to work looking like a different man. No smile. No light in his eyes.

"What's wrong, Billy?" I asked.

In a weak and tired voice, Billy explained that his teenage son, Byron, had gone to a local cowboy club with a few of his high school friends. He was one of two black kids in the place, but was enjoying the time with his buddies from school. Apparently, Byron left the club early, and as he walked to his car by himself, he was jumped by two tough-looking men. He was beaten badly. Billy said in a soft voice, "Byron came through the door with his face bloody, torn, and swollen. I was shocked and sickened. I kept thinking, *This isn't Texarkana, this is Thousand Oaks, California. How can this be?*"

Billy now had to say to his son what his own father once said to him. He opened up his Bible to Luke 6:27–28 and read the words of Jesus: "But I tell you who hear me: Love your enemies, do good to those who hate you, bless those who curse you, pray for those who mistreat you." The night of that tragedy Billy and Byron prayed together, recommitting themselves to love and not hate. To bless and not curse.

No doubt about it. Billy Burnett reflects the love of Jesus Christ, the kind of love that reaches out to red and yellow, black and white. The love that looks on the heart and not the outward appearance. He reflects the love of his Christian parents. And when he describes what life was like in Texarkana, both the sweet and the sad times, I am always moved to thank God for Christian mothers and fathers—folks like Willie and Mama Teal, parents who can make happy memories for their children even in a share-cropper's cabin.

Love is the mark of the Christian. Jesus Himself said, "By this all men will know that you are my disciples, if you love one another" (John 13:35). We don't have to want to do it. We don't have to feel loving. We are to love out of obedience to God.

> *We don't have to want to love. We don't have to feel loving. We are to love out of obedience to God.*

Last year, when Billy traveled to Africa with Wheels for the World, he came face-to-face with the life from which his people originally came. One day, as he was inspecting a facility with which Joni and Friends is partnering, he looked out the window. He stood for a moment and stared dreamily at the thick woods and distant fields. Suddenly, he saw something that made time stand still.

An African woman, with her hair covered in a brown-and-orange turban, was leaning over a wash bucket, scrubbing clothes in rhythm to a song she was humming. Billy's eyes filled with tears. "I saw my mother," he said. "So many years ago when I was a little boy, my mother would do the same. There in Africa, I was transported back to my sweet Texas, to a time when I helped my mother carry laundry, dig sweet potatoes, a time when I felt her embrace that morning I first went to the fields to pick cotton."

It was a picture of love all the way from America to Africa and back. And it's the love of his mother, father, and his God that Billy is committed to give wherever in the world God takes him.

We ought always to thank
God for you, brothers, and rightly
so, because your faith is growing
more and more, and the love
every one of you has for
each other is increasing.

2 THESSALONIANS 1:3

13

YET WILL I TRUST
HIM . . . AND GAIN AUTHORITY

*M*ost Christians, at one time or another, toy with the idea of becoming a missionary. Although I am a missionary of sorts as I sit in this wheelchair, and you, too, are in full-time Christian service as you share Christ at the office, in the neighborhood, or at school, there is something unique and precious about encountering a career missionary home on furlough from the mountainous outback of a forgotten country.

That's why I was so excited to spend an evening with my Dutch missionary friend, Gesina Blaauw. Fluent in Dutch, German, and Italian, Gesina had left Holland at a young age to work in a Christian bookshop in Italy

Gesina Blaauw

where she had hoped to begin a ministry to the Italians. But when people from Albania began walking through the front door, she started to ask questions. In broken Italian, they would answer, "We have left our country to escape the terrible persecution of President Hoxha. It is a horrible Communist regime!" Gesina would invite many to come back to her bookshop for more fellowship. It was also a chance to learn more about Albania, as well as to learn the Albanian language. Albania was a dangerous land where atheism was the official religion, yet Gesina sensed God calling her to serve as a missionary to the Albanian people.

"What was it like?" I asked. "Did you face persecution?"

Gesina's beautiful, cool blue eyes sparkled. She grinned and shook her head. "I will tell you a story of what I learned about persecution," she said. "My friends and I wanted very much to take Christian literature into Albania. There was one trip in particular when I was traveling alone—my friends did not know the route I was planning to take from Italy to Yugoslavia and then to the Albanian border. But it was a beautiful day and I was very happy," she said with a sigh. "That morning I had read Psalm 80:5 in my devotions where it said, 'You have fed them with the bread of tears.' I wasn't sure what the Lord was telling me. Maybe it was about feeding the Albanians the Word of God. I didn't know. I shrugged my shoulders and boarded the ferry for Yugoslavia.

"When we arrived in the area of Montenegro, I drove my Volkswagen off the ferry and proceeded to customs. In my car I had packed four Albanian New Testaments and a stack of John's gospels in the Albanian language, but I wasn't worried. That is, not until a customs officer began searching through my things. He even rummaged through my correspondence. When he read a letter in which I had written, 'We traveled through the Albanian part of Yugoslavia,' he was outraged. People in Montenegro hated the Albanians. He underlined these words and telephoned the local police. It seems I had offended national pride by calling parts of Yugoslavia Albanian.

"My Volkswagen was interned at the police station while I was hauled inside to be questioned. They sat me down in front of an Italian-speaking interrogator who fired questions at me like bullets. 'Why did you bring those books?' he demanded.

"'Because wherever in the world I am, this is the best gift I can give my friends.'

"'Why is that?'

"'Because this Book changed my life.'

"'How can a book change your life?'"

Gesina told me that she began to give her testimony to the officials. She got as far as describing her emptiness without Christ, at which point the police interrupted. "How did you get your car?!" to which she replied, "I needed a car and I prayed to God and He provided through the gifts of friends." They barked, "You are lying! And look at the kind of typewriter you have. It's an electric typewriter. With such sophisticated equipment, you must be spying."

The officials were getting more frustrated. Finally they said to her, "Do you understand that you are under arrest?"

Gesina said yes.

"How does that make you feel? Angry?"

Gesina said no.

"Aren't you afraid?"

Again, she said no.

"Then what do you want to learn?" the interrogator sneered.

In a voice laced with sweet peace, she replied, "I want to learn more from my Lord." Little did she realize that God was about to answer her request.

The officer who had acted as interpreter stepped up with handcuffs in his hand. "I'm sorry," he said apologetically, "but I have to do this. Do you want it on your left wrist or your right?" Gesina extended her left arm, and the officer clamped on one side of the handcuffs. The other he snapped to a leg of the desk. Then, without another word, the two men walked out, leaving Gesina alone, shackled to the desk.

They're just trying to scare me, Gesina thought. *They'll be back soon.*

But they didn't come back. More and more time passed, and still no one came. The handcuffs were cutting into her wrist, and still no one came. The sun grew dim and dusk darkened the room, and *still* no one came.

Hours later, two officers she had not seen before entered the totally dark room and offered Gesina milk and biscuits.

"What are your names?" Gesina asked between mouthfuls of biscuit.

"Sali," answered one. Gesina brightened. It was an Albanian name.

"Stephen," said the other. And a Christian name!

"Did you know your name is in the Bible?" Gesina asked

Stephen. "I can show you later." Then she spoke to Sali in his native Albanian language. Both men were friendly and kind, but they didn't unfasten her shackles. Neither did they leave.

Hours passed, and then Stephen said, "We really must take you down now."

"You mean downstairs? What's down there?"

"A bench and blankets," said Sali. "So you can sleep."

Lying down certainly did sound better than staying handcuffed to a desk. So why, Gesina wondered, did the two seem so reluctant to take her? As they started down the dark, narrow stairway, Gesina stumbled. Stephen took her arm and gently guided her. Between the dark and her missing glasses, Gesina couldn't see anything. But she was beginning to smell something, and it was not at all pleasant.

A metal door grated as it turned on its hinges and creaked open. Gesina was led into the basement cell, and the door clanged shut behind her. She was all alone in total darkness.

The unpleasant smell had grown into an overwhelmingly horrible stench. It was worse than a room full of rotten eggs. *Ugghh!* Gesina thought. *There must be human excrement all over this place!*

Still, she couldn't continue to stand in one spot all night. A bench to sleep on, the officers had said. Maybe if she could find that . . . Gingerly she felt her way over to it, and then carefully lay down. It had been an exhausting day. *They will let me go in the morning,* she assured herself. *All I have to do is make it through tonight.* Soon she fell into a restless sleep.

Hours later—Gesina had no idea how many—footsteps sounded through the barren walls. Someone was coming down the basement stairs. With a start, Gesina was fully awake. *Thank goodness! They've come to let me out.*

Then the clank of metal.

And the creaking swing of the cell door.

Finally a gruff command for her to step forward.

In the darkness, Gesina missed a step and fell awkwardly at the guard's feet. As she struggled to get up, the guard thrust a hunk of bread into one of her hands and a piece of salami into the other. Then the door slammed shut. Once again she was left alone in complete darkness.

With the slam of the door, Gesina's hopes evaporated. She was totally abandoned! No one in the whole world knew where she was. No one except the Lord God above. Only He could help her now.

With the bread in one hand and the salami in the other, Gesina stumbled back to the bench and slumped down. Hot tears filled her eyes and rolled down her cheeks. What was she going to do? She couldn't even eat her bread and salami! Not without one hand free so she could break off a bite. She certainly didn't dare put either one down. Not in the middle of . . . she hated to think about what was everywhere, yet she couldn't deny the source of the awful stench. Still clutching the food, she dropped both hands into her lap and sobbed. Tears streamed down her face and off her chin. They trickled down her neck and onto her dress.

Instinctively Gesina raised her right hand and wiped her tears with the tightly clutched hunk of bread.

Wait a minute! What was it she had read that very morning? *You have fed them with the bread of tears . . .*

The bread of tears! Gesina's mind reeled. *Jesus . . . His body . . . broken . . . crucified . . . for us!*

Bread of tears!

All God's people, through the centuries . . . one dough . . . made into one bread . . . mainly of tears!

Throughout history, suffering and persecution had been a regular part of most Christians' lives. And now here she was. She had become a part of them. No longer was she an outsider praying for the suffering church. No! She had become an honest-to-goodness participant. Now she could pray as an insider. She had the right to do so. She had gained the authority.

What freedom. What power. What joy.

So what did Gesina do? Immediately she put that new authority to work. Systematically and methodically she began to pray for the suffering church—country by country, government by government, region by region—in every part of the world. Never before had she interceded in the way she did all alone in that stench-filled basement cell.

Did the prison doors swing open and allow her to walk free? No. Did her suffering end? Hardly. Did others come to offer her support and encouragement? Not a one. No, the circumstances didn't change. But something was different. That something was Gesina herself.

"As I sat in the darkness of the filthy cell, I was suddenly singing to the Lord. As I worshiped Him, comfort flooded my soul and my heart united with His."

Her prayers had a new urgency . . . a new power. She prayed

and prayed and prayed. When she could stand the suffocating air no longer, she banged on the metal door until the guard grudgingly took her upstairs to the Turkish toilet. It was just a hole in the ground, but in comparison to the cell it was luxury. When she got back downstairs her energy was renewed, and she resumed her petitions to God on behalf of suffering Christians.

At one point during that day, someone else was pushed into the cell with her—a man who spoke no English or any other language she tried on him. It turned out that he was a Libyan terrorist, and he soon was taken away.

After three days, Gesina was finally taken to a courtroom where she was accused of offending the nationalistic identity of the Yugoslav people . . . and of being a spy for Albania . . . and of accepting payment from the Albanian government to spread propaganda against Yugoslavia. Her accuser stood over her and bellowed, "We have the last word here! You will never get out of prison. You will die there. Do you understand? You will die in prison!"

Gesina said nothing.

In the end, she was sentenced to thirty days.

The prison was in an entirely different area, far out in the countryside. How wonderful it was to get away from the disgusting basement cell. Gesina was taken into the women's quarters of the prison, then into the room she would share with six other women. The others stood perfectly still and silently watched as she was led in.

I am not going to allow myself any self-pity, she decided as she was pointed to her bed without a mattress. *This will be a time of growing fellowship with the Lord. He can bless me even here. He can use me even in prison.*

She met her new roommates: an attempted murderess, several thieves. The others didn't volunteer their crimes, but it was safe to say no one else was imprisoned for their love of Christ. No watches were allowed, so the only clue to the time of day was the arrival of meals and the change of the guards. No books were allowed. No activities either. Nothing but boredom.

As the days wore on, bitterness and contention grew between the women. One woman was a spiritist medium, and she would lay out cards to tell the others their future. Gesina tried hard to tell the other women of God's love. She tried to explain that the fortune-telling was from Satan and that it formed a barrier between them and God.

They just laughed at her.

As we suffer for Christ, He blesses us with greater authority in prayer, in study, and in our witnessing.

Then Gesina had an idea. As the others worshiped Satan through their actions, she worshiped the Lord God. *This spiritual battle,* she determined, *will be fought in the heavenly places!* She climbed up on a chair, and from there onto the windowsill where she could hold on to the bars. In that position she was high enough to look out over the prison walls and see the glimmering starry sky. Right in front of her beamed the brightest of the stars—the polar star. Clinging to the bars, she gazed out at that star and sang songs of worship to the Lord.

"Nothing else mattered, Joni," Gesina told me. "Not the room, not the prison, not the other prisoners. It was just the Lord and me. He filled me with incredible joy and peace. We were so close! Our fellowship was so precious!"

As Gesina sang, the women got out their fortune-telling cards and called out, "Look, Gesina! Satan!"

But they liked the singing. Or, as Gesina insists, they enjoyed the taste of an atmosphere permeated with the Lord's peace. Now and then, if they thought Gesina might not sing, they asked her to climb up to the bars and start her serenade. One night she really didn't feel like it. As the time wore on, the women became more and more quarrelsome, and more and more nasty to one another until it was almost unbearable. *All right,* Gesina decided. *I will sing, whether I want to or not. I will sing to the Lord, I will sing for the others, and I will sing for myself.*

Many days passed for Gesina in that prison. Many nights, too. Little did she realize that while she was standing on the chair under the windowsill, holding on to the iron bars and singing songs of worship into the night sky, her friends in Italy and Yugoslavia were praying. These same friends realized that something had run afoul when Gesina did not answer her phone and had not shown up at a prearranged meeting. They tried to piece together her route, guessing which road she would have taken through the twists and turns of the coast of Montenegro. They got in their cars and drove back and forth, stopping to ask questions, searching the parking lots, talking to Christians along the way.

Finally, when Gesina's friends were near exhaustion, they

turned into the police station at the little ferry town on the coast. There, behind a high chain-link fence, they saw a sight that made them gasp. It was Gesina's Volkswagen! They recognized the color and the stickers!

In the next few hours, phone calls were made, embassies were contacted, officials were notified, and Gesina's Christian friends marched into the police station with all the official documentation they needed to secure her release. By the next morning, the prison doors flung open for Gesina, and she stumbled into the arms of her brothers and sisters in Christ. After many tears, hugs, and kisses, the small group stepped back from Gesina. Something about her seemed . . . different.

It was at that point I interrupted my Dutch missionary friend. "I know what was different," I said. Gesina gave me a funny look. "It was your new authority in Christ."

"You're exactly right, Joni," she said with a smile. "And it's something I feel so privileged to have. I am not an outsider where it concerns the fellowship of sharing in Christ's sufferings. Not that I have tasted the sort of persecution our brothers in the Sudan or Indonesia must suffer, but what little I have experienced has taught me that God releases power and infuses energy into the lives of those whose tears are their bread. As we suffer for Christ, He blesses us with greater authority in prayer, in study, and in our witnessing."

I looked at my paralyzed legs and hands. I guess you could say that I "suffer" for Christ in that I look to Him for grace and strength. And, true, I have experienced that wide-open, bold, happy confidence in the Lord Jesus as I trust Him in my afflictions, which affects everything from how I pray to the way I wake up in the morning. But there is something *more* in Gesina's life. Any of us can gain that same degree of authority she enjoys. Indeed, if we live for Christ in our neighborhoods and at work, we *will* face persecution—whether at the watercooler or a cold shoulder across the backyard fence.

Gesina Blaauw had to leave America to return to Albania the week after we were together. She is laboring in a free country—at least, freer than it was under Communism. But Albania is still steeped in abject poverty and economic ruin. There are refugees from Kosovo and Bosnia to tend to. There are hate and crime, corruption, malnutrition, and orphans begging on the streets. You can find Gesina celebrating her authority in Christ as she traipses up the mountains north of Tiranë to show the *Joni* movie or the *Jesus* film on a battery-operated projector that shows the image on a sheet stretched between two poles. You can find Gesina giving food to the poor, clothes to the children, medicine to the sick, mattresses to the homeless, and Bibles to everyone.

> *God releases power and infuses energy into the lives of those whose tears are their bread.*

And everyone who passes under her wise and happy touch learns to love her Jesus. They can't help it. She's got that kind of authority.

In all these things we are more than conquerors through him who loved us.

⌐◦

ROMANS 8:37

14

By Faith, in Faith, and Through Faith

*I*n my travels, I've met many extraordinary people with exemplary faith and, yes, some of them are people whose names you know. Like Billy and Ruth Graham or Presidents Reagan and Bush. I could have written about individuals like these, but there was a reason I chose the people in this book.

They are like you.

Their names aren't household words. They haven't written books or spoken to thousands, and only one has traveled the world. Yet their lives are enjoying a powerful influence on the people they meet. But why do we stop and take notice of someone like Barbie Kolar or Joan Liggins, Gesina Blaauw or Billy Burnett? Because of their *stories*.

You see, there might be some individuals whose lives seem a little bland, like vanilla pudding. But when such a person is suddenly disadvantaged—whether through disability, death, or deep disappointment—a new element is introduced. The hero of the story has become hobbled, so he or she has much less chance of winning. No one would blame the story's hero if he gave up. But if he overcomes in spite of the odds and by the grace of God, well . . . *that's* what makes the story powerful, important, and truly worth reading.

All through the Bible God shows us that this is exactly the

Sharing my faith in Christ

way He likes to do things. He allows disadvantages to encroach on our lives in order to bring maximum glory to Himself while the hero is made more heroic. The apostle Paul told the Corinthian Christians to look around at themselves. He asked them to see that, on the whole, God called people into their fellowship who, by human standards, were neither wise nor important nor famous. He was saying that God deliberately chooses unlikely, ill-equipped, problem-riddled people to get His work done. Why? So that when the challenges are overcome, everyone looking on will know that everything was accomplished by God's grace: the persever-ance, the long-suffering, the hope, the ability to wait, the love and patience, and, yes, even the smile.

God allows disadvantages to encroach on our lives in order to bring maximum glory to Himself while the hero is made more heroic.

Like I said, this is you. You with your own special set of challenges and disappoint-ments. And if it's not you, it could be. The way you approach life's difficulties can and should have a weighty influence on everyone around you. All it takes is faith.

When you receive that bad medical report or you are the object of others' abuse or scorn, when your reputation is unfairly slandered or you are confronted with a life-altering disability, you are driven to your knees in weakness and frailty. You are driven there not only *by* faith, but *in* and *through* faith. *By faith* because you have nowhere else to turn. *In faith* because you must trust the One who holds your hardships in His hands. *And through faith* because you are able to rise from your knees and go forth in hope and confidence.

The apostle Paul, who had his own set of challenges, explains this beautifully in 2 Corinthians 12:9–10:

> But he said to me, "My grace is sufficient for you, for my power
> is made perfect in weakness." Therefore I will boast all the more
> gladly about my weaknesses, so that Christ's power may rest on
> me. That is why, for Christ's sake, I delight in weaknesses, in
> insults, in hardships, in persecutions, in difficulties. For when I
> am weak, then I am strong.

Incredible. Delight in weaknesses? With God, even *that's* possible.

God may not show you all the answers and, like Barbie Kolar, you may never know the answers. Even though the Lord does not spread before you the blueprint of your life, explaining His plans and purposes, you can still come to Him by faith. Why? Because most, if not all, of God's answers are found at Calvary. Begin by dropping to your knees before the cross of Christ and laying all your questions at Jesus' feet. Yield any stiff-necked, stubborn rebellion—call it sin, if you will—that you might have toward Him. In so doing, you'll discover the answer that will suffice for all your hurts.

It is Christ who, with His blood, has paid the penalty of His own Father's judgment against your sin and, as you yield your life, it is Christ who will be the Author and Perfecter of your faith. Despite all your unanswered questions, you will receive the goal of your faith—the salvation of your soul (1 Peter 1:9). What freedom! What peace!

Ask Jesus Christ to forgive your doubts and fears. Ask Him to take away any sin that separates you from Him. Then rise in faith and move forward into your life through faith in the One who gave His life for you. In the One who works all things together for your good and His glory.

It only takes faith the size of a mustard seed to do this. But—hey—give God an inch, and He'll take a mile, encouraging and

> *Give God an inch, and He'll take a mile, encouraging and strengthening you each step of the way.*

strengthening you each step of the way. By His grace, He will enable you to delight in your weaknesses, to overcome in spite of the odds. And you will be the true hero of your own story . . . the hero He always intended you to be.

And the happy ending? It's coming sooner than you think.

"For I know the plans I have for you,"

    declares the LORD,

"plans to prosper you

    and not to harm you,

    plans to give you hope and a future.

Then you will call upon me

    and come and pray to me,

    and I will listen to you.

You will seek me and find me when you

    seek me with all your heart.

I will be found by you,"

    declares the LORD.

—JEREMIAH 29:11–14

Notes

Chapter 4

1. "Gonna Go to Heaven" by Ron Krueger and David
   Mullen © 1996 Word Music and Seat of the Pants
   Music. International rights secured. All rights reserved.
   Reprinted with permission. Do not duplicate.

Chapter 6

1. Used by permission. "Journey's End" © 1978 by
   Robert Tregenza for the *Joni* movie.

Chapter 8

1. Maria Garriott, "Hoop Dreams and Hard Realities,"
   Baltimore Sun, 18 May 1995.

ACKNOWLEDGMENTS

Special Thanks To . . .

My friends at Thomas Nelson, especially Janet Thoma, for giving birth to the idea for *Ordinary People, Extraordinary Faith* several years ago. Thank you, Janet, for investing so much energy into the creation of this special book.

Kay Marshall Strom—for lending me her time, organizational skills, and expertise in not only writing several of the chapters, but in serving as my main cheerleader. Bless you, Kay, for being the foreman on this project.

Robert Wolgemuth—for always going to bat for me. You and Janet put your heads together and—voila!—we were on our way, writing up a storm.

Francie Lorey—for serving as my hands at the computer. Thank you for your tireless dedication to helping me and your devotion to serving the Lord.

My fifteen friends—you may think your lives are ordinary, but your love for Jesus Christ and your enthusiasm for kingdom advancement inspire more people than you realize. Thank you for allowing me to share your stories with many more new friends in hopes that all of us, myself included, will follow Christ more nearly and love Him more dearly.

About the Author

Most of the people Joni has written about in this book are men, women, and children she has encountered through the ministry of Joni and Friends. After Joni became a quadriplegic as a result of a diving accident in 1967, she began to share how God was the key to accepting her disability. Then after she wrote her autobiography, *Joni*, this young woman in a wheelchair began receiving letters from people all over the world. To adequately respond to the many needs and questions, Joni formed the Christian organization Joni and Friends in 1979.

For more than twenty years, Joni and Friends has

been dedicated to extending the love of Christ to people who are affected by disability. Joni Eareckson Tada leads a team of staff and volunteers throughout the United States and around the world who make it their goal to meet the physical, emotional, and spiritual needs of disabled people and their families.

From local neighborhoods to the far reaches of the world, Joni and Friends seeks to equip and mobilize churches to carry out the work of disability ministry. Every year, JAF holds Family Retreats that involve hundreds of families affected by disability, and nearly as many staff and volunteers. Wheels for the World, another program of Joni and Friends, mobilizes volunteers to collect used but serviceable wheelchairs in order to refurbish them and ship them overseas to needy disabled people in developing nations. Teams of Christian physical therapists raise their own support to travel with Wheels for the World, helping to fit each wheelchair to the individual needs of disabled children and adults. Bibles are distributed and disability ministry training is held in local churches.

Joni and her husband, Ken, reside in Calabasas, California, where they invest a great deal of time in the work of Joni and Friends. For more information about all the programs of Joni and Friends, or if you wish to contact Joni and Ken, we invite you to write:

Joni and Friends
P.O. Box 3333
Agoura Hills, CA 91376
818/707-5664 • TTY: 818/707-9707
www.joniandfriends.org